mini FOR ORGANS, PIANOS & ELECTRONIC KEYBOARDS

2 E-Z PLAY TODAY

BEST OF BEATLES

80 _____ HITS

ISBN 978-1-4950-7719-7

HAL•LEONARD®

7777 W. BLUEMOUND RD. P.O. BOX 13819 MILWAUKEE, WI 53213

Visit Hal Leonard Online at
www.halleonard.com

CONTENTS

4

All My Loving

Registration 9
Rhythm: Rock

Words and Music by John Lennon
and Paul McCartney

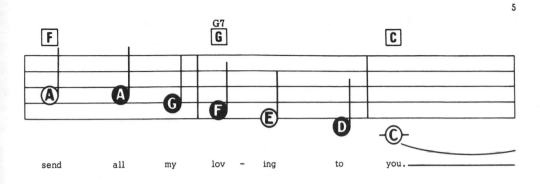

send　　　all　　　my　　lov - ing　　　　to　　　you.＿＿＿＿＿

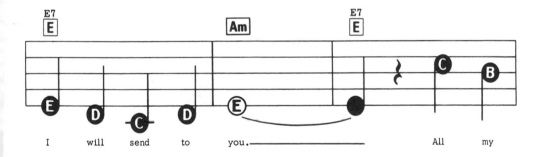

＿＿＿　I'll　pre -　＿＿＿　All　my　lov - ing,

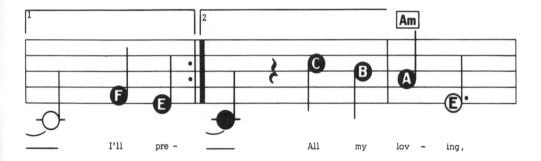

I　will　send　to　you.＿＿＿＿＿＿＿＿＿＿　All　my

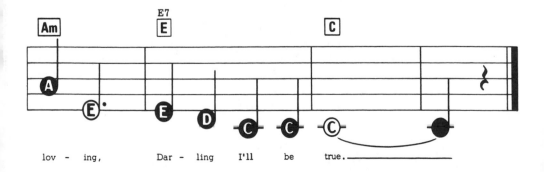

lov - ing,　Dar - ling　I'll　be　true.＿＿＿＿＿

All You Need Is Love

Registration 5
Rhythm: Shuffle or Swing

Words and Music by John Lennon
and Paul McCartney

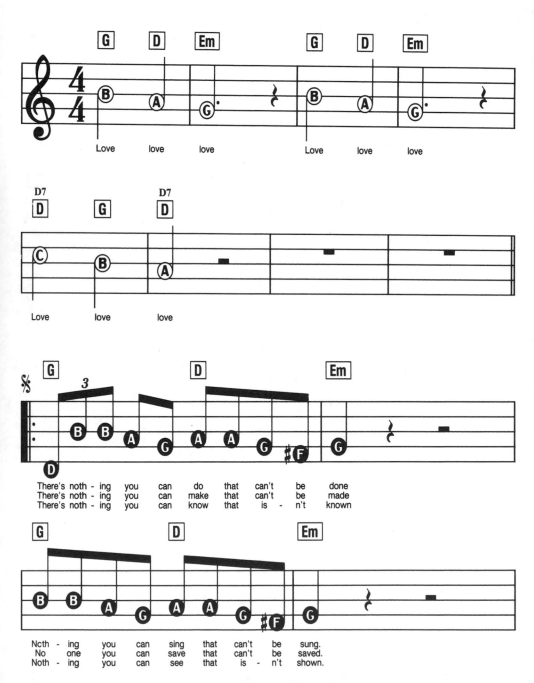

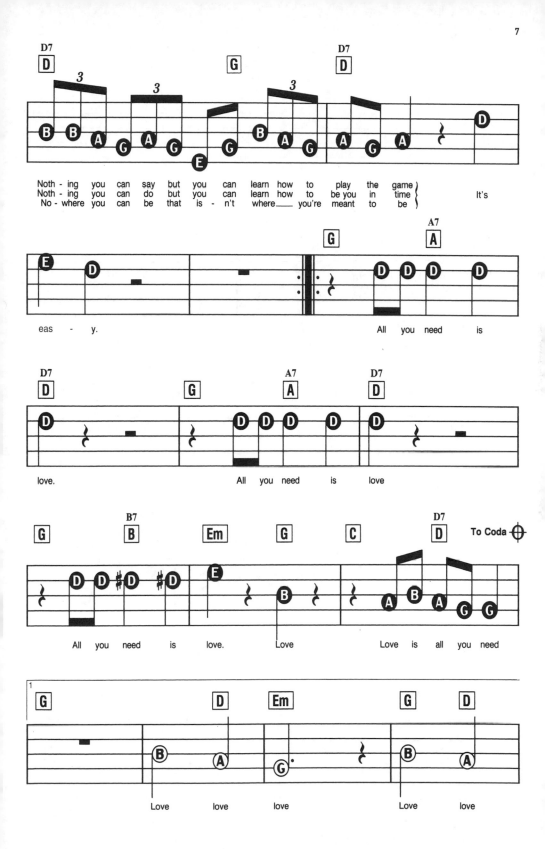

8

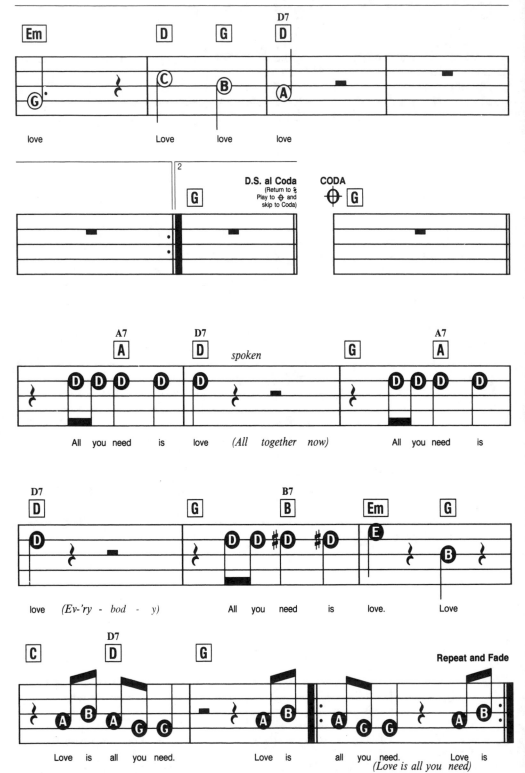

And Your Bird Can Sing

Registration 8
Rhythm: 8 Beat or Rock

Words and Music by John Lennon
and Paul McCartney

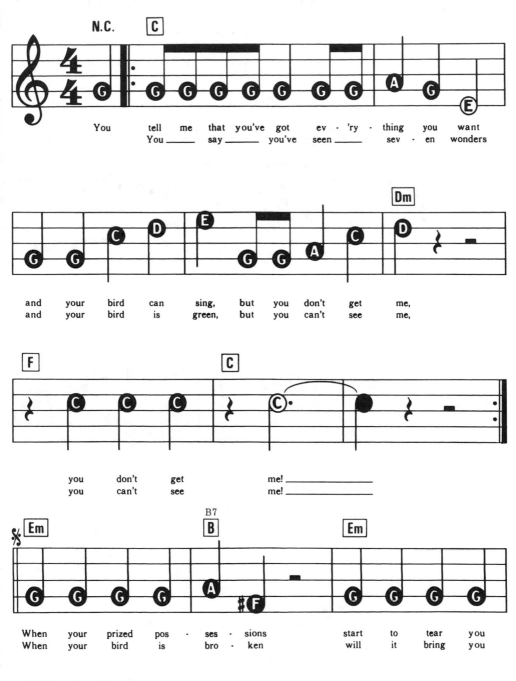

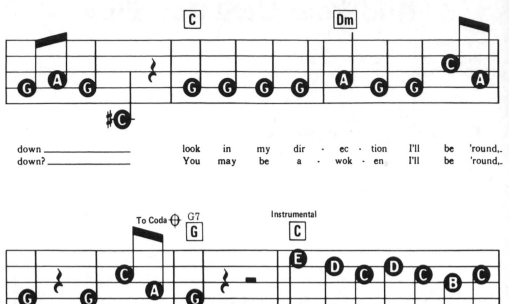

down _____ look in my dir · ec · tion I'll be 'round,
down? _____ You may be a · wok · en I'll be 'round,

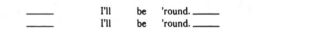

_____ I'll be 'round. _____
_____ I'll be 'round. _____

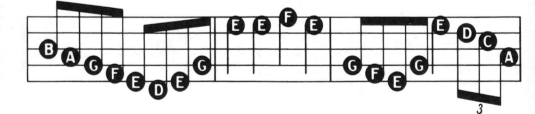

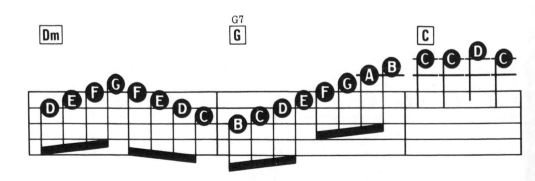

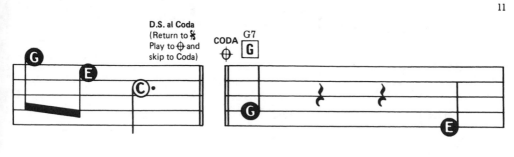

D.S. al Coda
(Return to 𝄋
Play to ⊕ and
skip to Coda)

CODA

_____ You

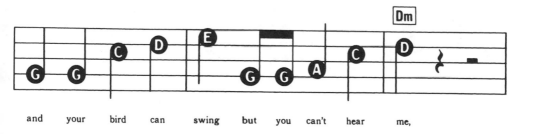

tell me that you've heard ev - 'ry sound there is

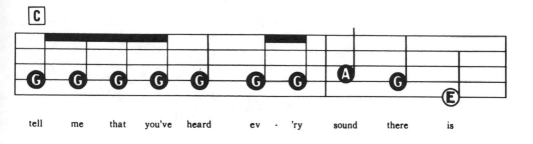

and your bird can swing but you can't hear me,

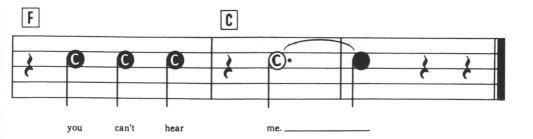

you can't hear me. _____

And I Love Her

Registration 8
Rhythm: Rock or Jazz Rock

Words and Music by John Lennon
and Paul McCartney

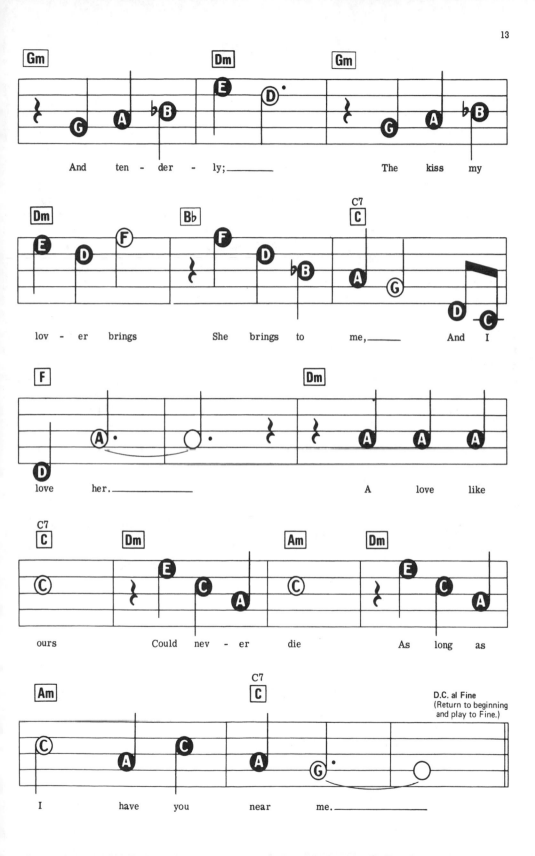

Back in the U.S.S.R.

Registration 4
Rhythm: Rock or Jazz Rock

Words and Music by John Lennon
and Paul McCartney

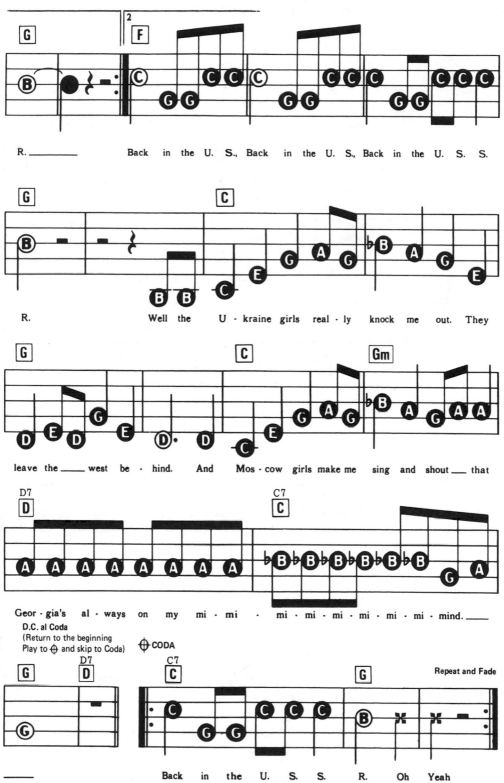

R. _____ Back in the U. S., Back in the U. S., Back in the U. S. S.

R. Well the U - kraine girls real · ly knock me out. They

leave the ____ west be · hind. And Mos · cow girls make me sing and shout __ that

Geor · gia's al · ways on my mi · mi - mi · mi · mi · mi · mi · mi · mind. ____

D.C. al Coda
(Return to the beginning
Play to ⊕ and skip to Coda)   ⊕ CODA

Repeat and Fade

_____ Back in the U. S. S. R. Oh Yeah

Because

Registration 1
Rhythm: Rock or Jazz Rock

Words and Music by John Lennon
and Paul McCartney

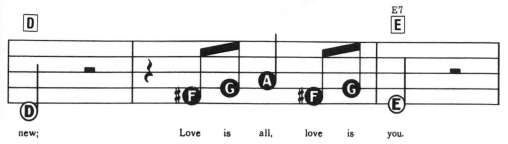

new;   Love   is   all,   love   is   you.

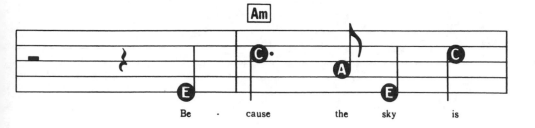

Be - cause   the   sky   is

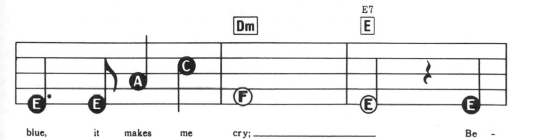

blue,   it   makes   me   cry; _____ Be -

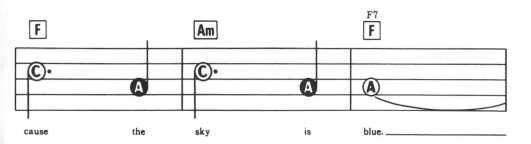

cause   the   sky   is   blue. _____

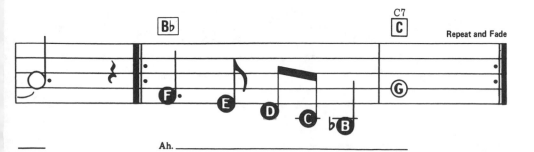

_____   Ah. _____

Birthday

Registration 2
Rhythm: Rock

Words and Music by John Lennon
and Paul McCartney

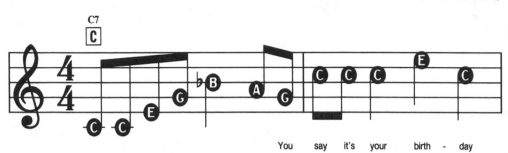

You say it's your birth - day

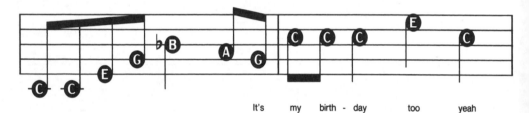

It's my birth - day too yeah

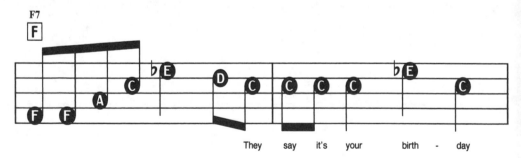

They say it's your birth - day

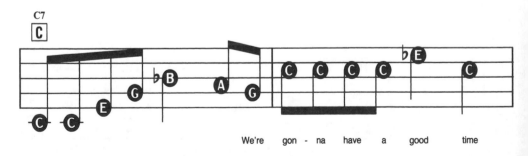

We're gon - na have a good time

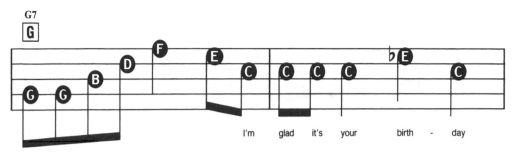

I'm glad it's your birth - day

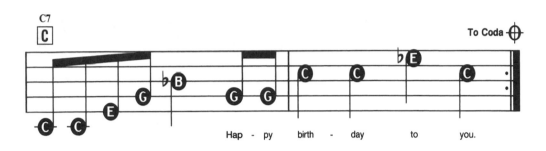

Hap - py birth - day to you.

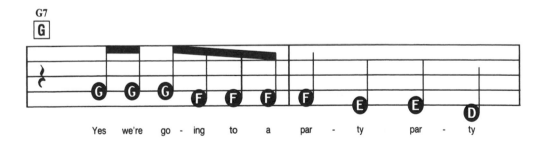

Yes we're go - ing to a par - ty par - ty

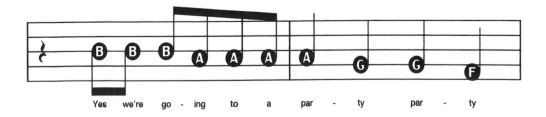

Yes we're go - ing to a par - ty par - ty

22

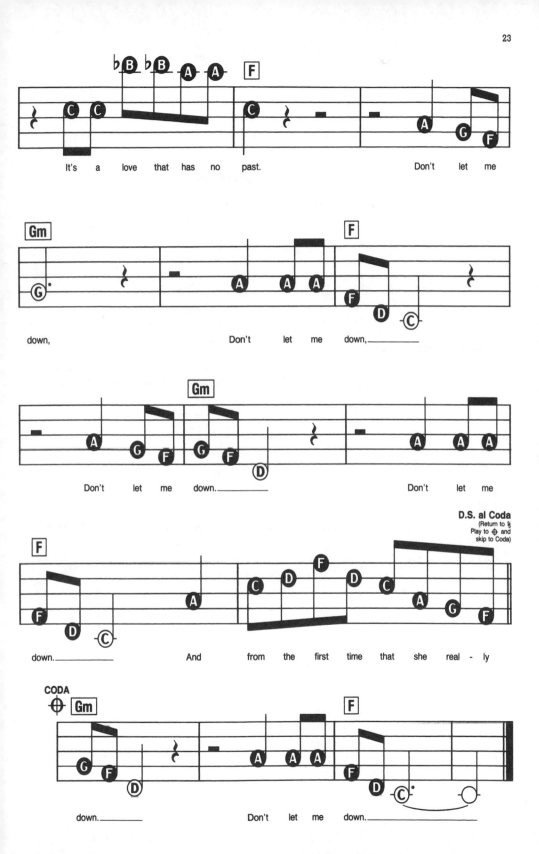

Blackbird

Registration 8
Rhythm: Rock

Words and Music by John Lennon
and Paul McCartney

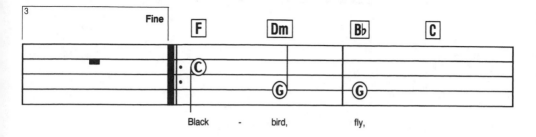

Black - bird, fly,

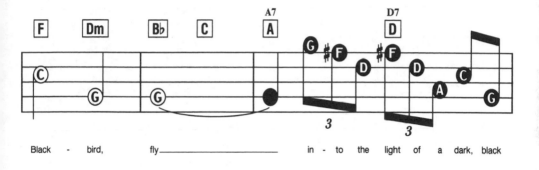

Black - bird, fly_____ in - to the light of a dark, black

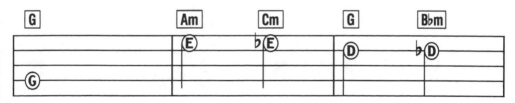

night. *Instrumental*

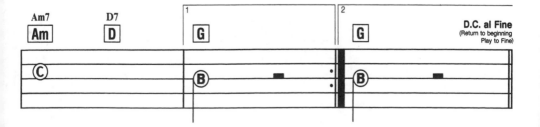

Can't Buy Me Love

Registration 1
Rhythm: Rock

Words and Music by John Lennon
and Paul McCartney

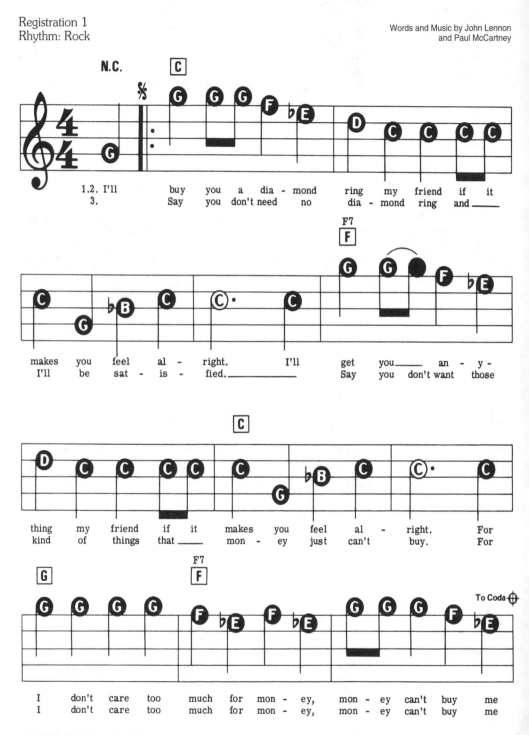

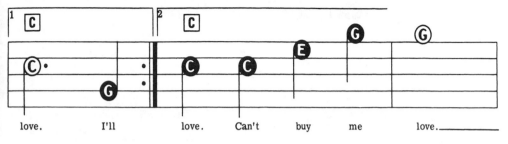

love.   I'll   love.   Can't   buy   me   love.

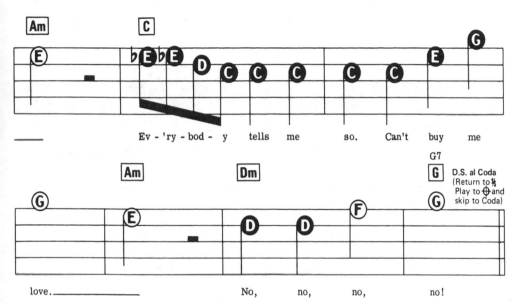

Ev - 'ry - bod - y   tells   me   so.   Can't   buy   me

love.   No,   no,   no,   no!

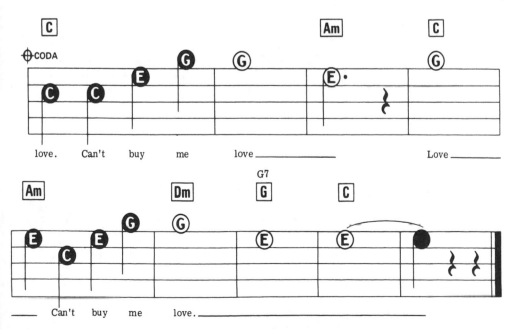

love.   Can't   buy   me   love   Love

Can't   buy   me   love.

Come Together

Registration 9
Rhythm: Rock

Words and Music by John Lennon
and Paul McCartney

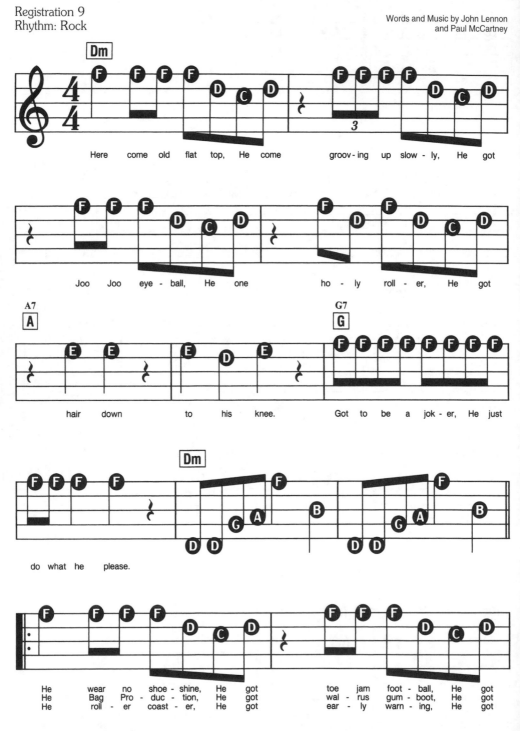

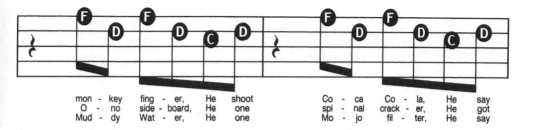

mon - key fing - er, He shoot
O - no side - board, He one
Mud - dy Wat - er, He one

Co - ca Co - la, He say
spi - nal crack - er, He got
Mo - jo fil - ter, He say

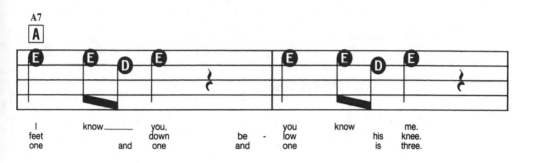

A7

I know_____ you,
feet down
one and one

you know me.
be - low his knee.
and one is three.

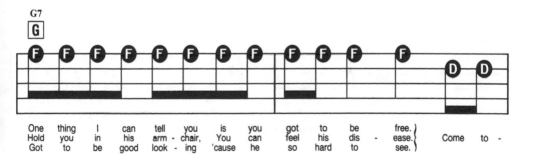

G7

One thing I can tell you is you got to be free.
Hold you in his arm - chair, You can feel his dis - ease.
Got to be good look - ing 'cause he so hard to see.

Come to -

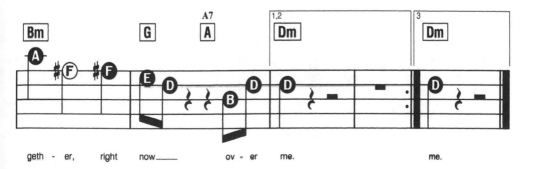

Bm   G   A7
                    A
                         1,2
                         Dm
                              3
                              Dm

geth - er, right now_____ ov - er me.   me.

A Day in the Life

Registration 2
Rhythm: Rock

Words and Music by John Lennon
and Paul McCartney

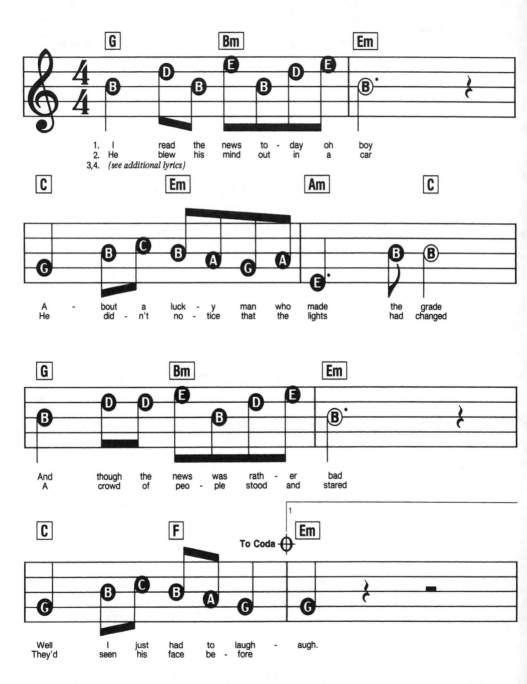

31

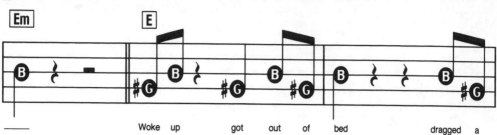

Woke up got out of bed dragged a

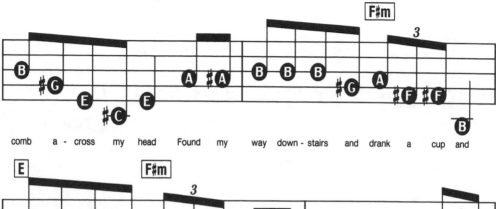

comb a - cross my head Found my way down - stairs and drank a cup and

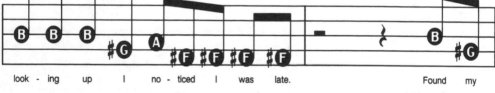

look - ing up I no - ticed I was late. Found my

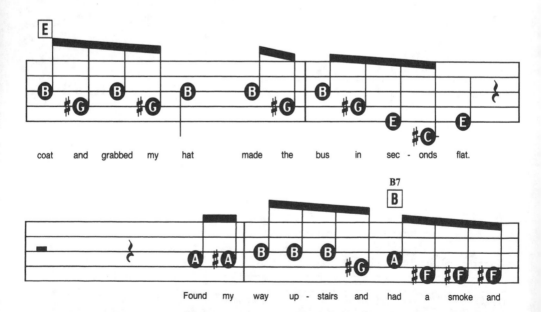

coat and grabbed my hat made the bus in sec - onds flat.

Found my way up - stairs and had a smoke and

D.S. al Coda
(Return to beginning
Play to ⊕ and
skip to Coda)

some - bod - y   spoke   and   I   went   in - to   a   dream.

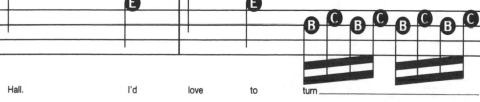

Now   they   know   how   man - y   holes   it   takes   to   fill   the   Al - bert

Hall.   I'd   love   to   turn_____

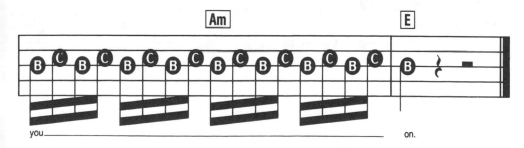

you_____   on.

3. I saw a film today oh boy
   The English army had just won the war
   A crowd of people turned away
   But I just had to look

4. I heard the news today oh boy
   Four thousand holes in Blackburn Lancashire
   And though the holes were rather small
   They had to count them all

Day Tripper

Registration 2
Rhythm: Rock or Disco

Words and Music by John Lennon
and Paul McCartney

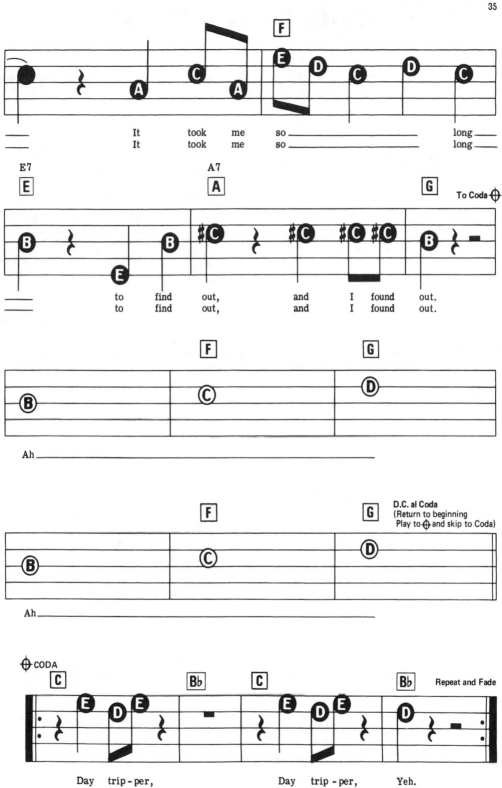

It took me so _____ long ___
It took me so _____ long ___

E7

A7

To Coda

___ to find out, and I found out.
___ to find out, and I found out.

F

G

Ah _____

F

G

D.C. al Coda
(Return to beginning
Play to ⊕ and skip to Coda)

Ah _____

⊕ CODA

C   B♭   C   B♭   **Repeat and Fade**

Day trip-per,   Day trip-per, Yeh.

Eight Days a Week

Registration 2
Rhythm: Rock

Words and Music by John Lennon
and Paul McCartney

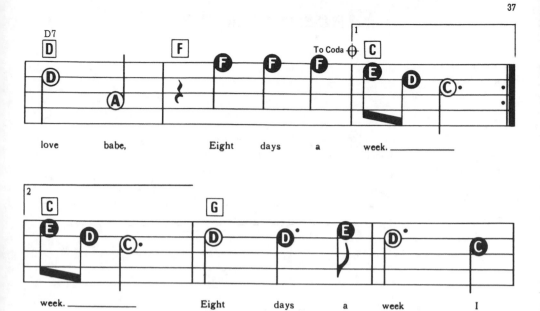

love babe, Eight days a week.

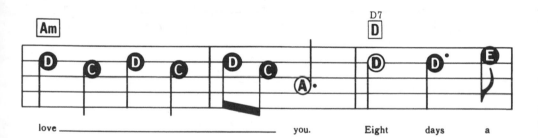

week. Eight days a week I

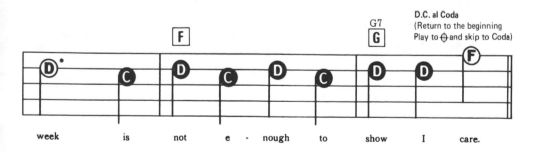

love you. Eight days a

D.C. al Coda
(Return to the beginning
Play to ⊕ and skip to Coda)

week is not e - nough to show I care.

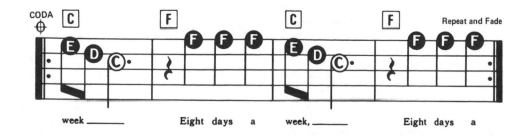

Repeat and Fade

week Eight days a week, Eight days a

Eleanor Rigby

Registration 9
Rhythm: Rock

Words and Music by John Lennon
and Paul McCartney

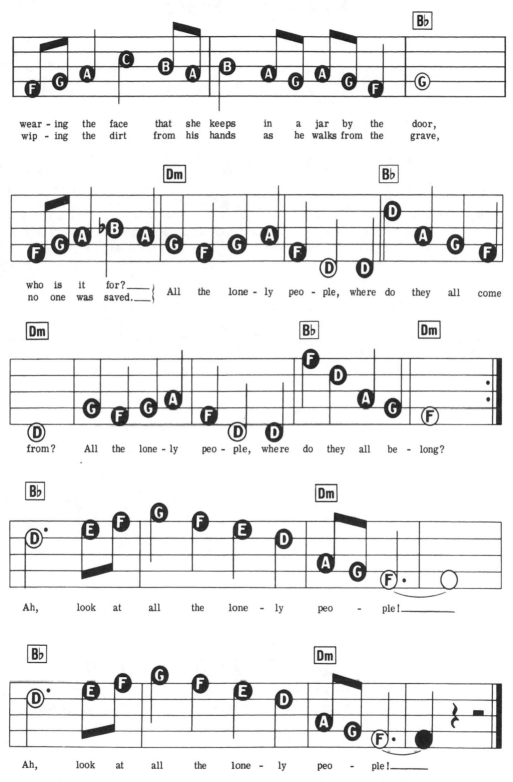

Fixing a Hole

Registration 2
Rhythm: Rock or Jazz Rock

Words and Music by John Lennon
and Paul McCartney

41

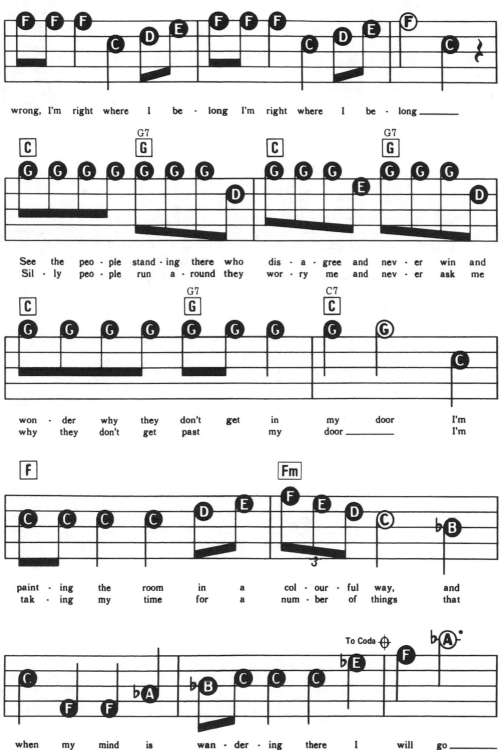

42

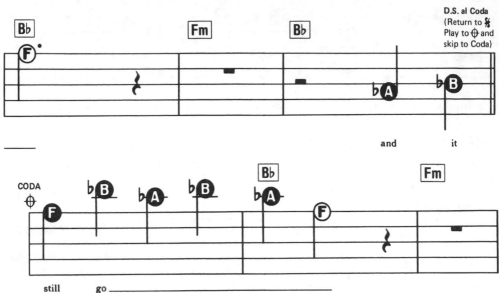

and it

still go _____

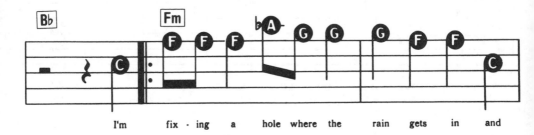

I'm fix · ing a hole where the rain gets in and

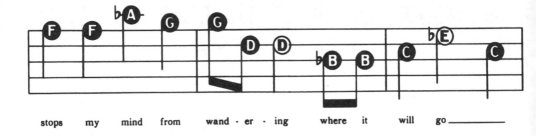

stops my mind from wand · er · ing where it will go _____

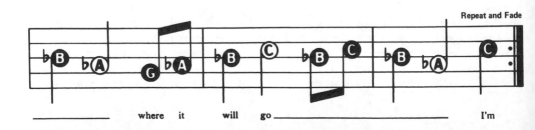

_____ where it will go _____ I'm

Good Day Sunshine

Registration 5
Rhythm: Shuffle or Swing

Words and Music by John Lennon
and Paul McCartney

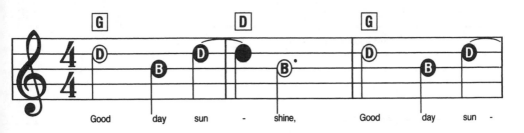

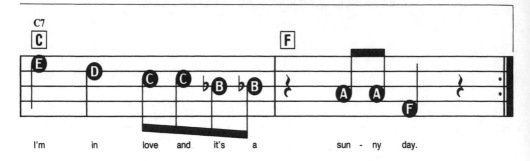

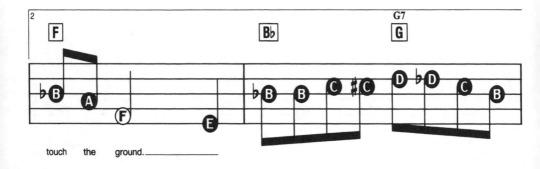

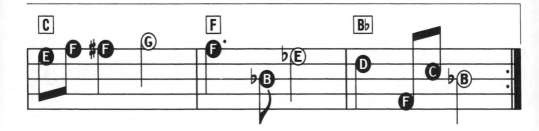

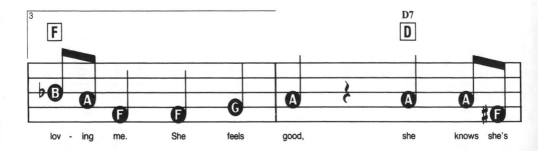

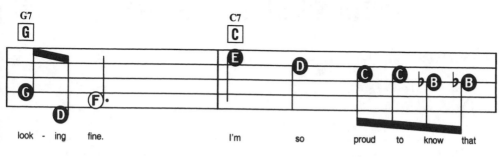

look - ing fine. I'm so proud to know that

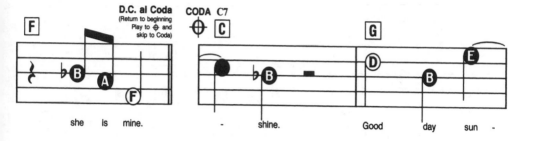

she is mine. - shine. Good day sun -

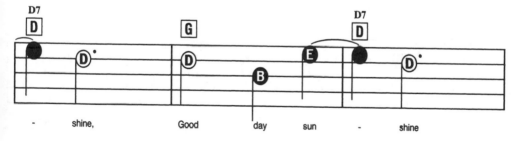

- shine, Good day sun - shine

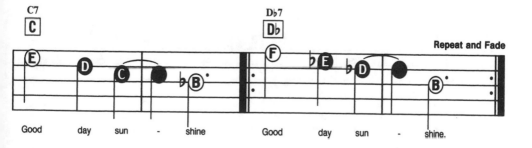

Good day sun - shine Good day sun - shine.

The Fool on the Hill

Registration 1
Rhythm: Rock or Bossa Nova

Words and Music by John Lennon
and Paul McCartney

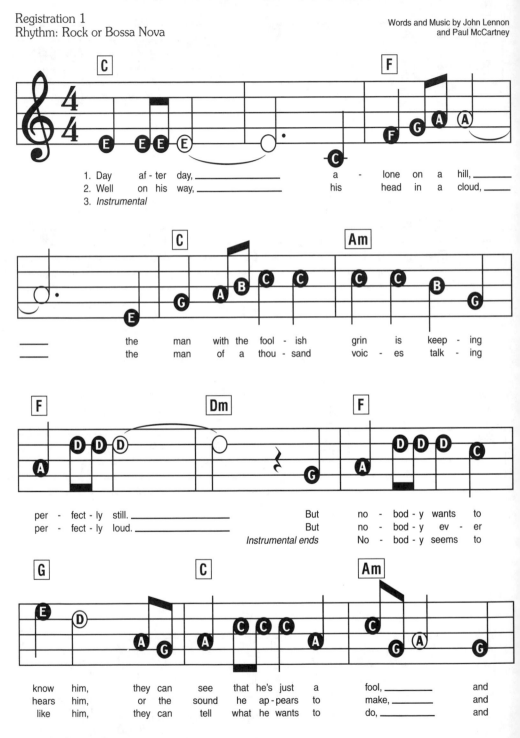

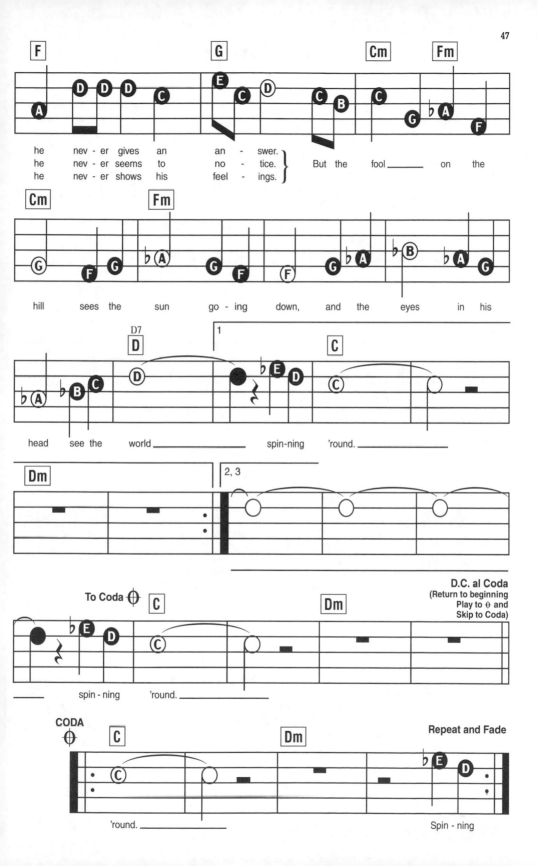

Get Back

Registration 8
Rhythm: Rock

Words and Music by John Lennon
and Paul McCartney

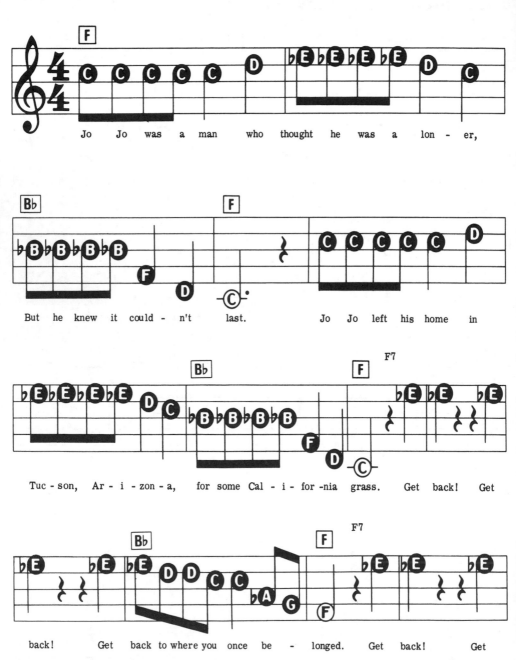

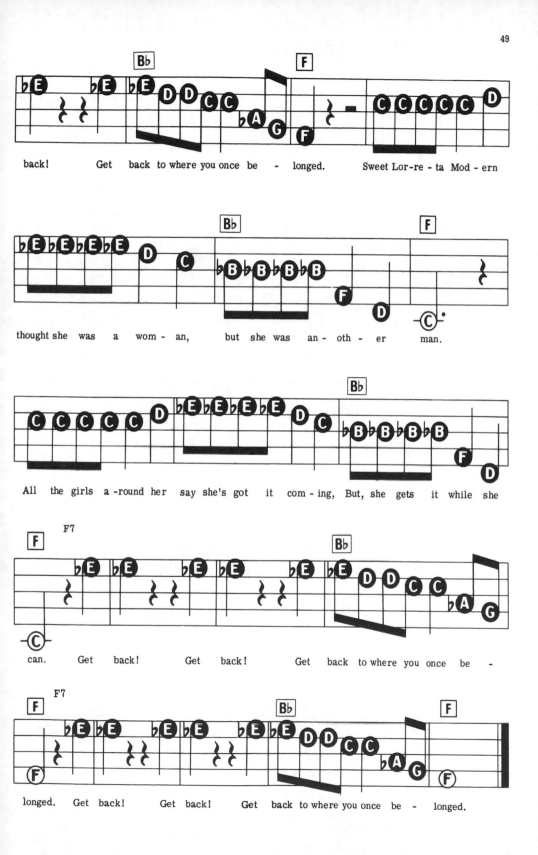

Good Night

Registration 3
Rhythm: Ballad

Words and Music by John Lennon
and Paul McCartney

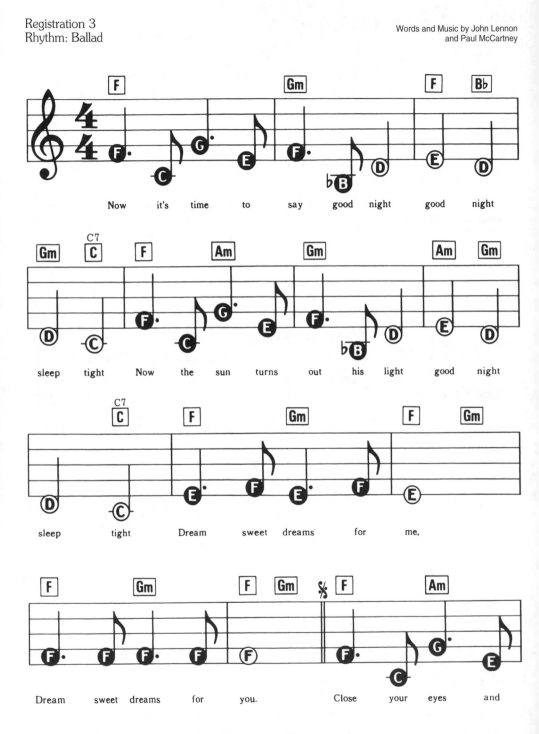

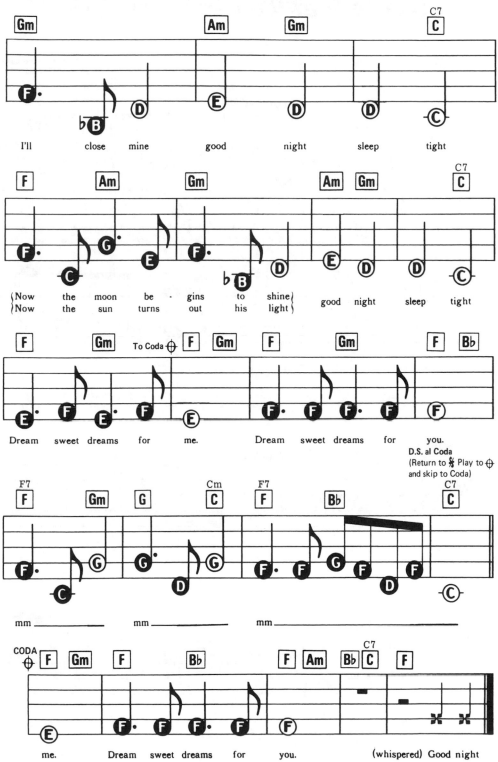

Got to Get You Into My Life

Registration 9
Rhythm: Rock or Jazz Rock

Words and Music by John Lennon
and Paul McCartney

I was a - lone, I took a ride I did - n't know what I would
You did - n't run, you did - n't lie you knew I want - ed just to

find there An - oth - er road, where may - be
hold you And had you gone you knew in

I could see an - oth - er kind of life there.
time we'd meet a - gain for I'd have told you.

Ooh, then I sud - den - ly see you. Ooh, did I
Ooh, you were meant to be near me. Ooh, and I

tell you I need you ev - 'ry sin - gle
want you to hear me say we'll be to-

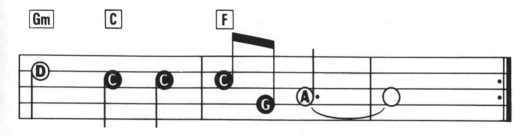

day of my life? _____
gether ev - 'ry day. _____

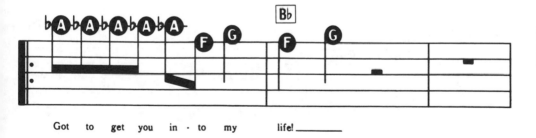

Got to get you in - to my life! _____

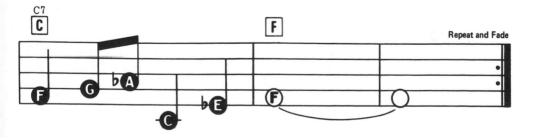

Repeat and Fade

A Hard Day's Night

Registration 7
Rhythm: Rock or Jazz Rock

Words and Music by John Lennon
and Paul McCartney

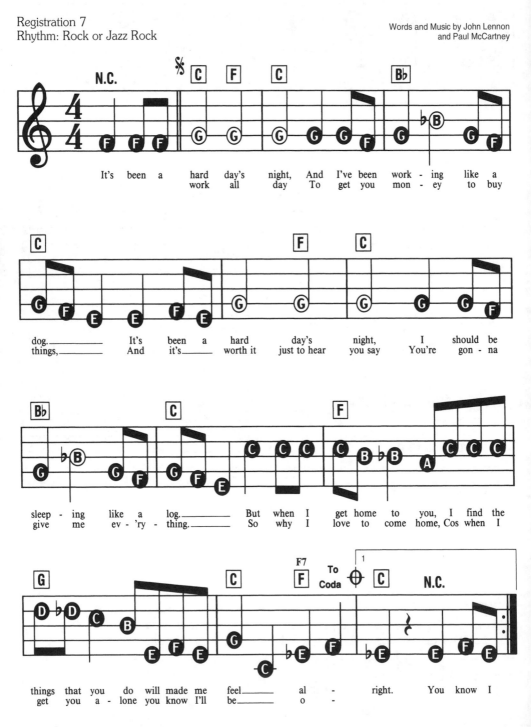

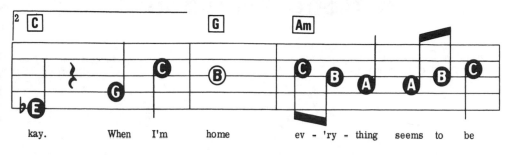

kay.   When   I'm   home   ev - 'ry - thing   seems   to   be

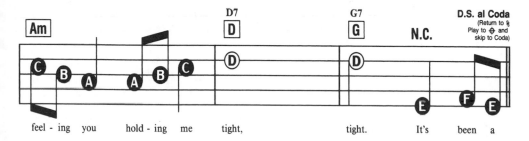

right._____   When   I'm   home

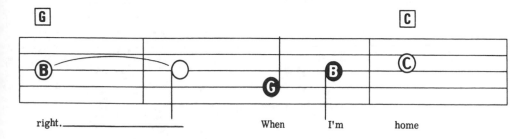

feel - ing   you   hold - ing   me   tight,   tight.   It's   been   a

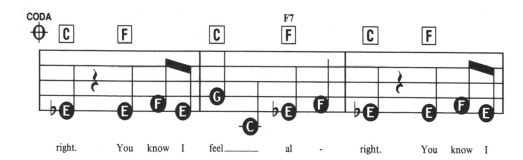

right.   You   know   I   feel____   al - right.   You   know   I

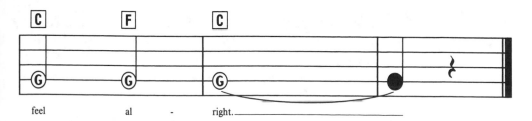

feel   al - right._____

Hello, Goodbye

Registration 3
Rhythm: Rock or Latin Rock

Words and Music by John Lennon
and Paul McCartney

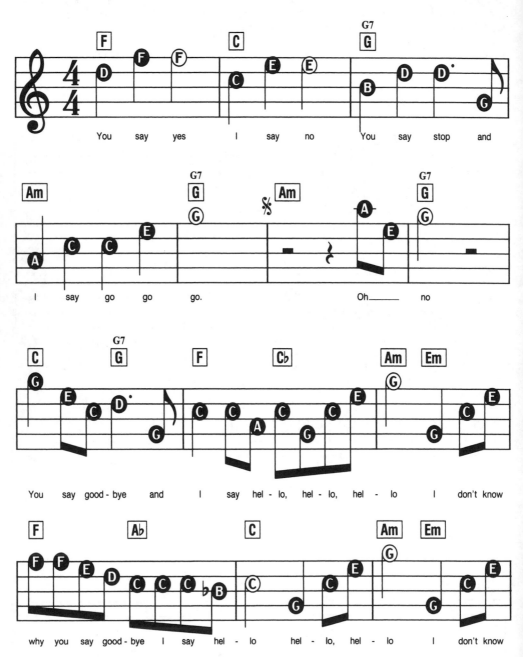

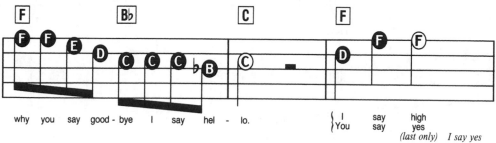

why you say good-bye I say hel-lo.　{ I say high / You say yes } *(last only) I say yes*

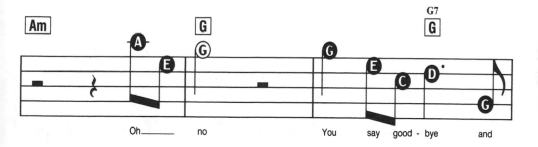

You say low　I say no / *But I may mean no*　You say why / *You say stop*　and　I say　and I can stay —　I don't know / *till it's time to go.*　{ *Oh* — }

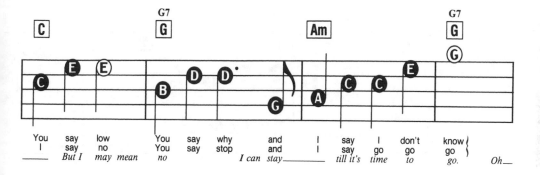

Oh — no　　You say good-bye and

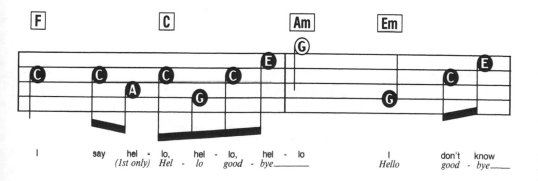

I　say hel-lo, hel-lo, hel-lo / *(1st only) Hel-lo good-bye* —　　I / *Hello*　don't know / *good-bye* —

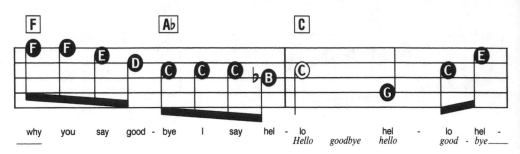

why you say good - bye I say hel - lo
Hello goodbye hello lo hel -
good - bye

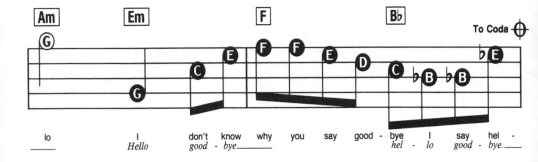

lo I
Hello don't know why you say good - bye I say hel -
good - bye *hel - lo good - bye.*

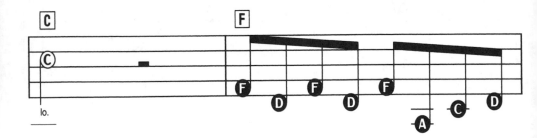

lo.

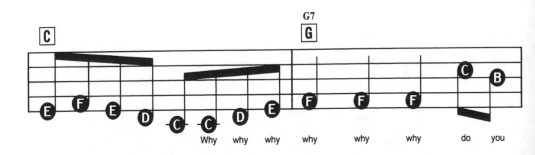

Why why why why why why do you

59

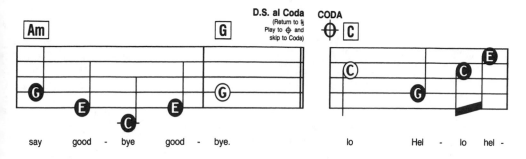

say good - bye good - bye.
lo   Hel - lo hel -

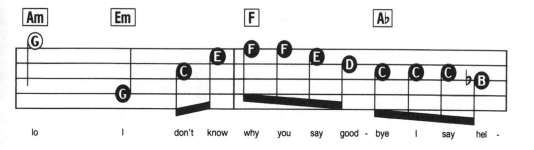

lo   I   don't know why you say good - bye I say hel -

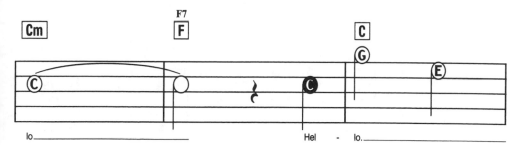

lo_____ Hel - lo._____

Repeat and Fade

He - la he - ba___ hel - lo - a.

Help!

Registration 3
Rhythm: Rock or Jazz Rock

Words and Music by John Lennon
and Paul McCartney

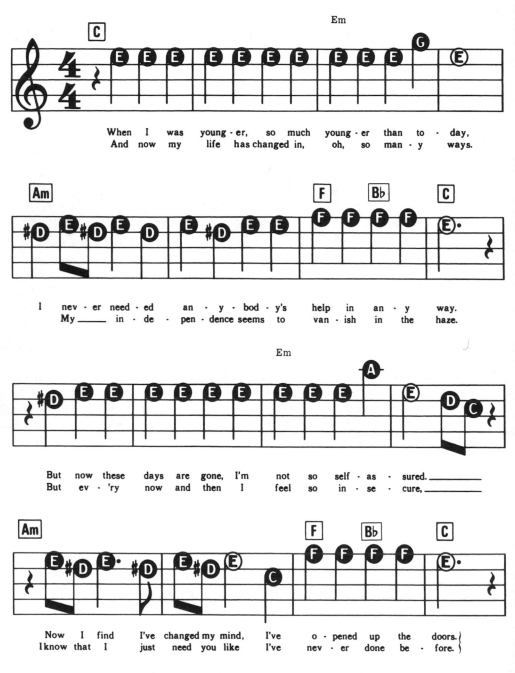

When I was young-er, so much young-er than to-day,
And now my life has changed in, oh, so man-y ways.

I nev-er need-ed an-y-bod-y's help in an-y way.
My in-de-pen-dence seems to van-ish in the haze.

But now these days are gone, I'm not so self-as-sured.
But ev-'ry now and then I feel so in-se-cure,

Now I find I've changed my mind, I've o-pened up the doors.
I know that I just need you like I've nev-er done be-fore.

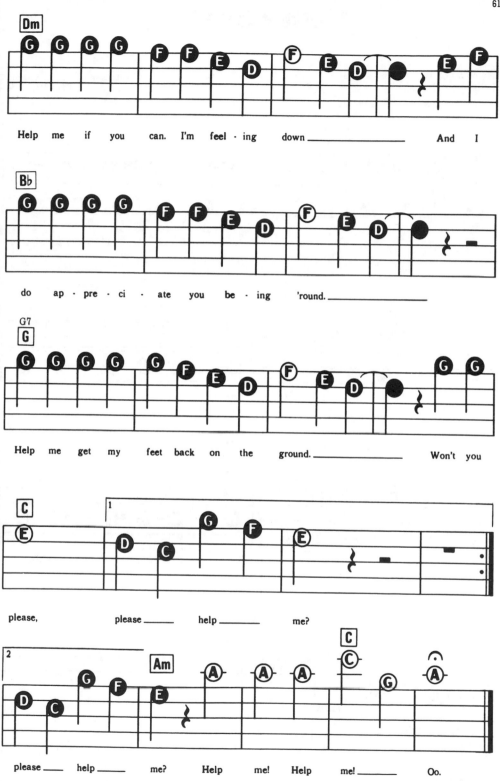

Helter Skelter

Registration 4
Rhythm: Rock

Words and Music by John Lennon
and Paul McCartney

G

shout

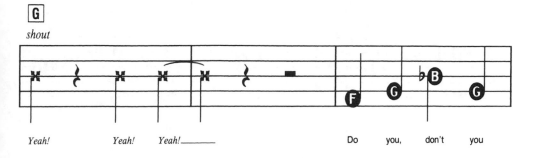

Yeah!   Yeah!   Yeah!___   Do   you,   don't   you

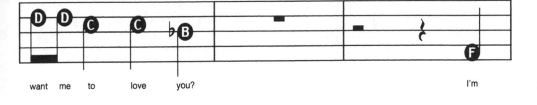

want   me   to   love   you?   I'm

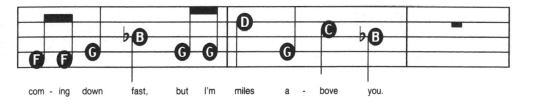

com - ing   down   fast,   but   I'm   miles   a - bove   you.

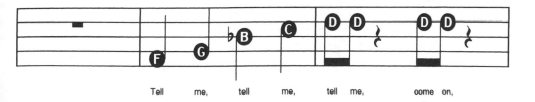

Tell   me,   tell   me,   tell   me,   come on,

64

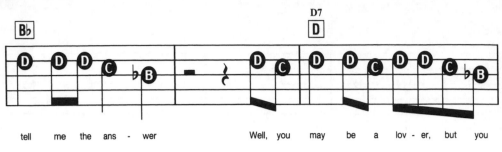

tell me the ans - wer Well, you may be a lov - er, but you

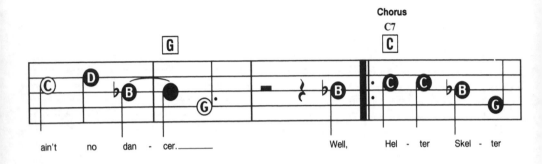

ain't no dan - cer._____ Well, Hel - ter Skel - ter

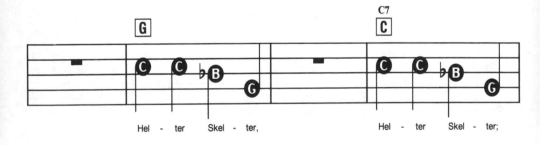

Hel - ter Skel - ter, Hel - ter Skel - ter;

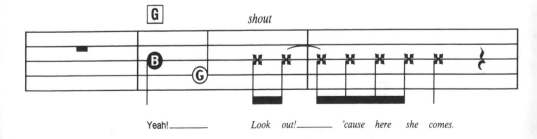

Yeah!_____ *Look out!*_____ *'cause here she comes.*

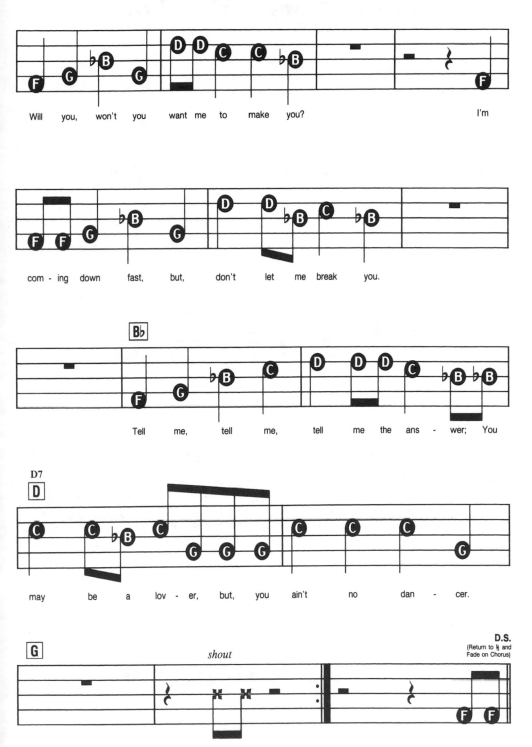

Here Comes the Sun

Registration 7
Rhythm: Rock

Words and Music by
George Harrison

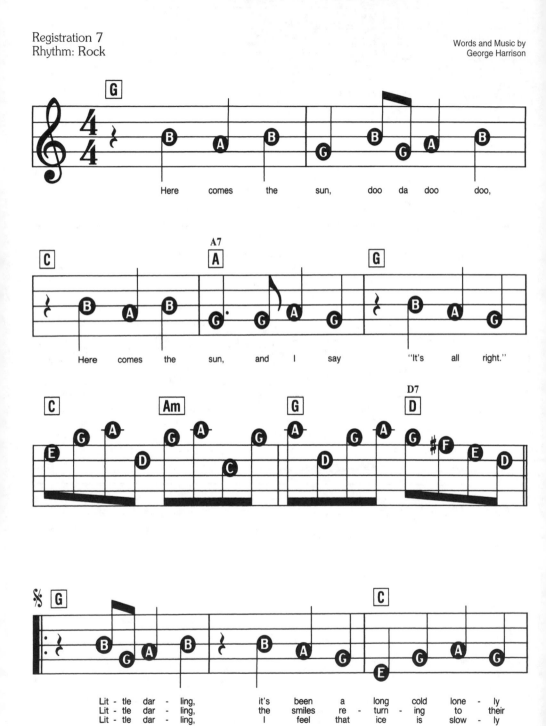

Here comes the sun, doo da doo doo,

Here comes the sun, and I say "It's all right."

Lit - tle dar - ling, it's been a long cold lone - ly
Lit - tle dar - ling, the smiles re - turn - ing to their
Lit - tle dar - ling, I feel that ice is slow - ly

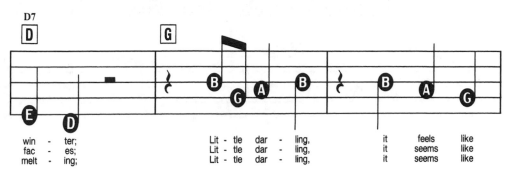

win - ter;
fac - es;
melt - ing;

Lit - tle dar - ling,
Lit - tle dar - ling,
Lit - tle dar - ling,

it feels like
it seems like
it seems like

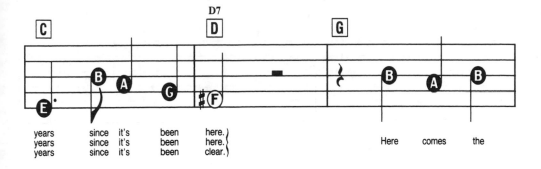

years since it's been here.
years since it's been here.
years since it's been clear.

Here comes the

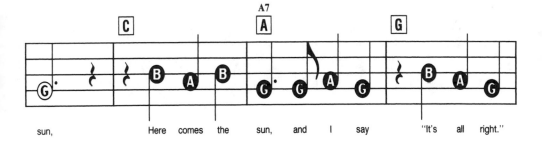

sun,

Here comes the sun, and I say "It's all right."

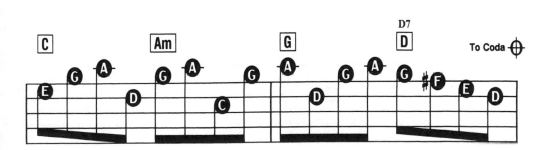

68

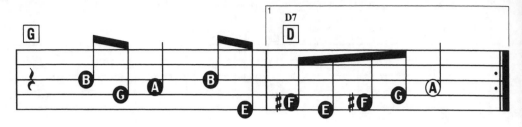

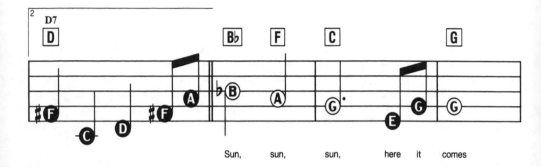

Sun, sun, sun, here it comes

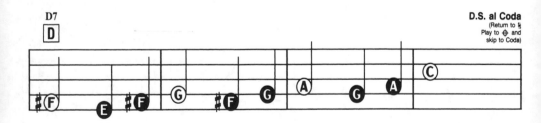

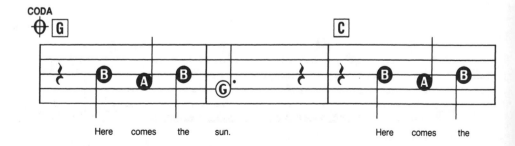

Here comes the sun. Here comes the

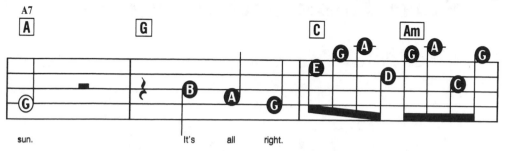

sun.   It's   all   right.

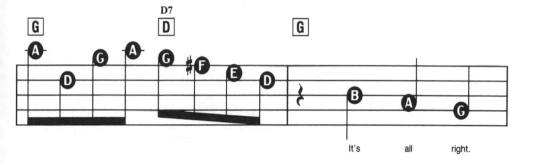

It's   all   right.

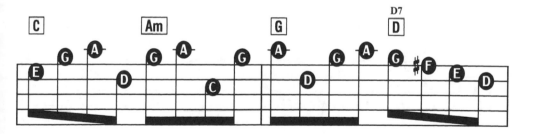

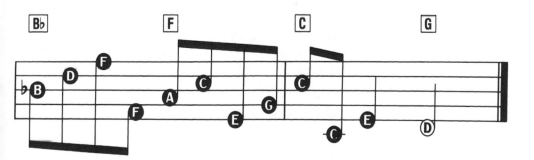

Here, There and Everywhere

Registration 2
Rhythm: 8 Beat or Rock

Words and Music by John Lennon
and Paul McCartney

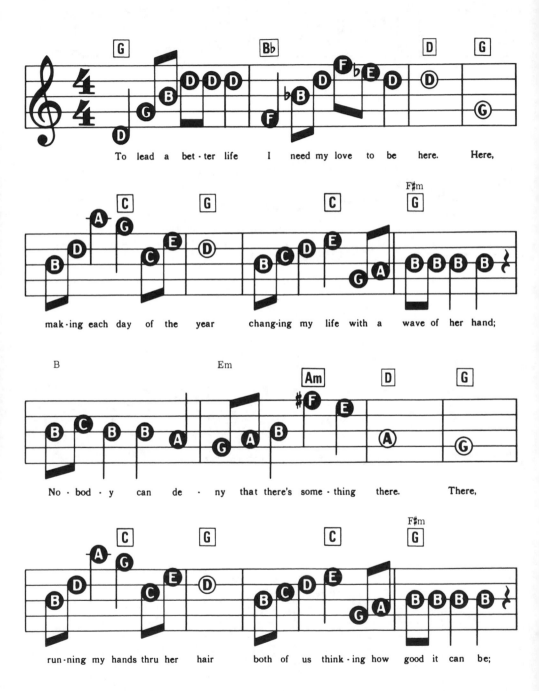

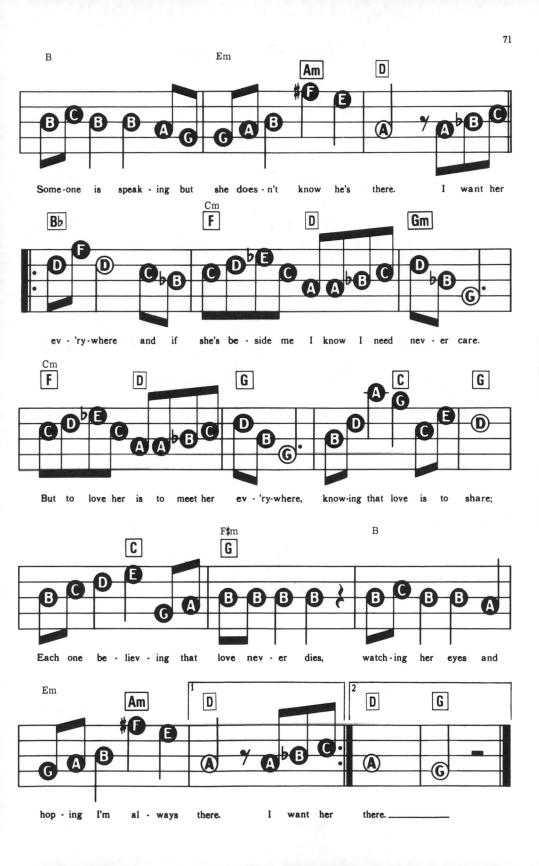

71

Hey Bulldog

Registration 8
Rhythm: 8 Beat or Rock

Words and Music by John Lennon
and Paul McCartney

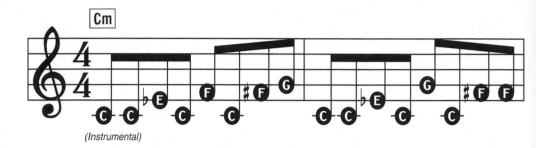

(Instrumental)

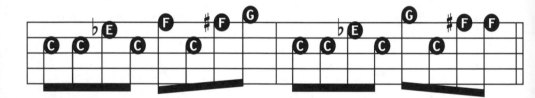

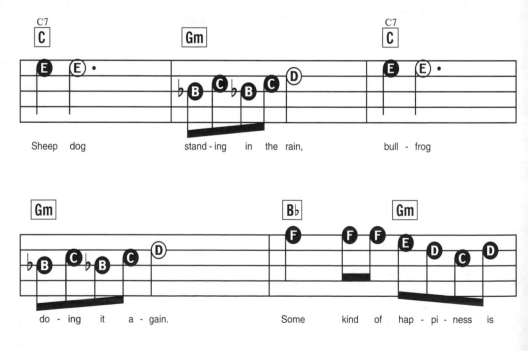

Sheep dog   stand - ing   in   the rain,   bull - frog

do - ing it a - gain.   Some   kind   of hap - pi - ness is

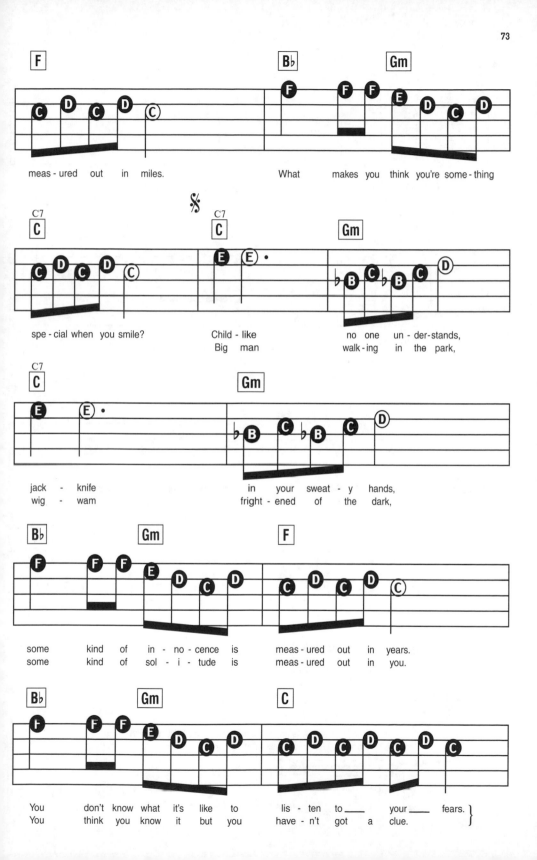

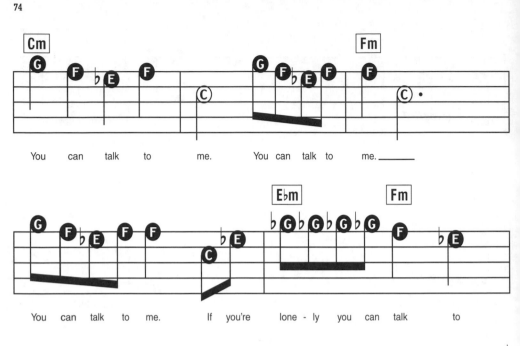

You can talk to me. You can talk to me. _____

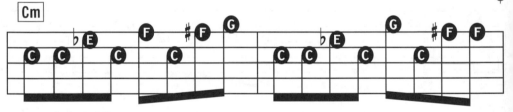

You can talk to me. If you're lone - ly you can talk to

To Coda ⊕

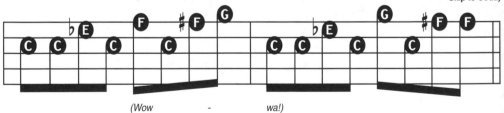

me. *(Instrumental)*

D.S. al Coda
(Return to 𝄋
Play to ⊕ and
Skip to Coda)

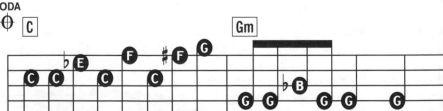

(Wow - wa!)

CODA

Hey bull -

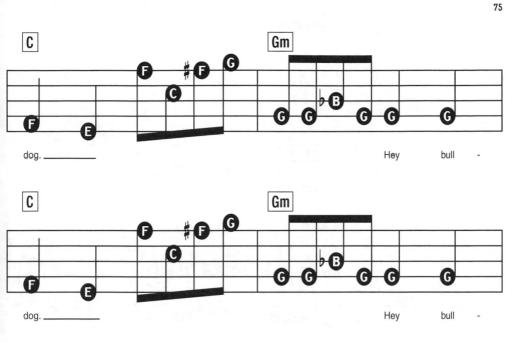

dog. _____ Hey bull -

dog. _____ Hey bull -

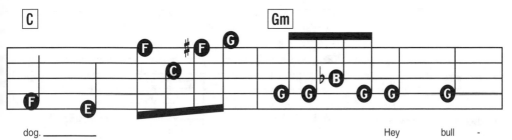

dog. _____ Hey bull -

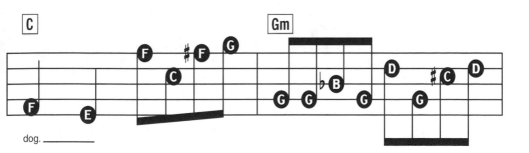

dog. _____

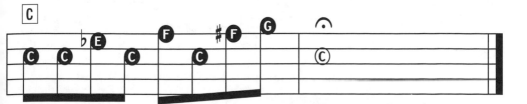

Hey Jude

Registration 2
Rhythm: Pops or 8 Beat

Words and Music by John Lennon
and Paul McCartney

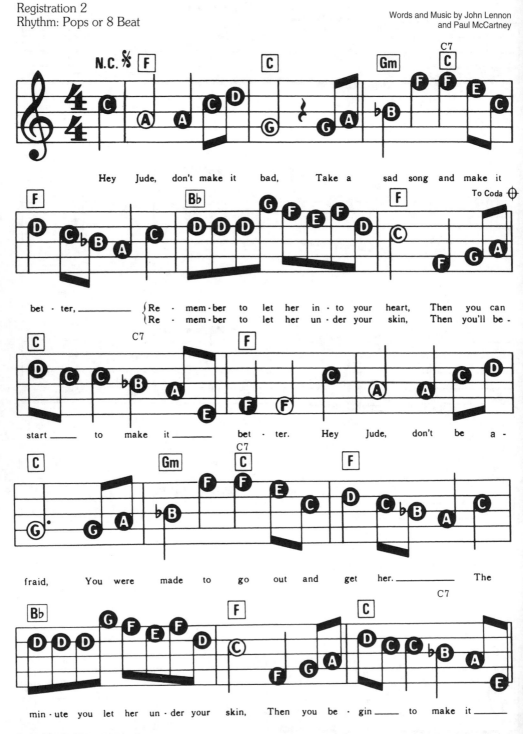

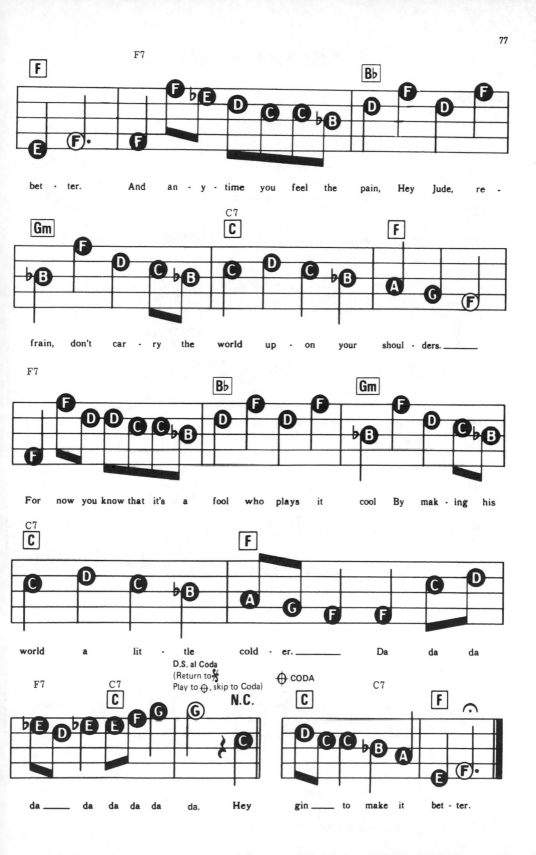

I Am the Walrus

Registration 5
Rhythm: Rock

Words and Music by John Lennon
and Paul McCartney

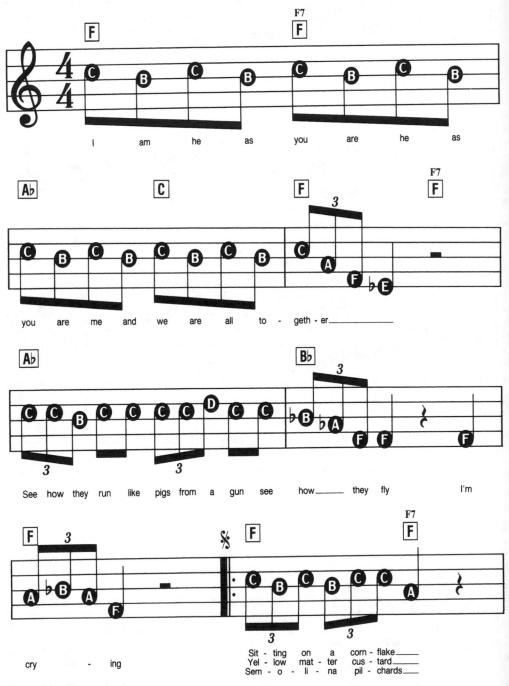

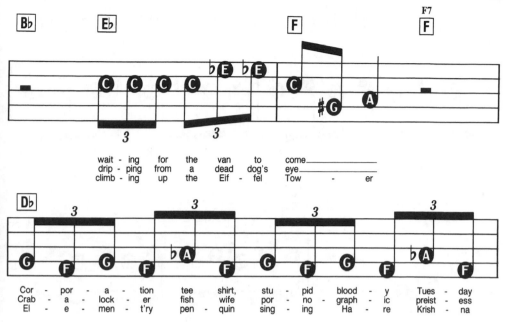

wait - ing for the van to come_____
drip - ping from a dead dog's eye_____
climb - ing up the Eif - fel Tow - er

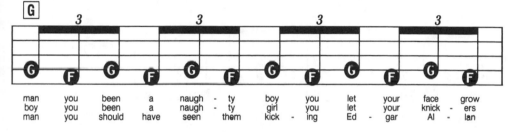

Cor - por - a - tion tee shirt, stu - pid blood - y Tues - day
Crab - a - lock - er fish wife por - no - graph - ic preist - ess
El - e - men - t'ry pen - quin sing - ing Ha - re Krish - na

man you been a naugh - ty boy you let your face grow
boy you been a naugh - ty girl you let your knick - ers
man you should have seen them kick - ing Ed - gar Al - lan

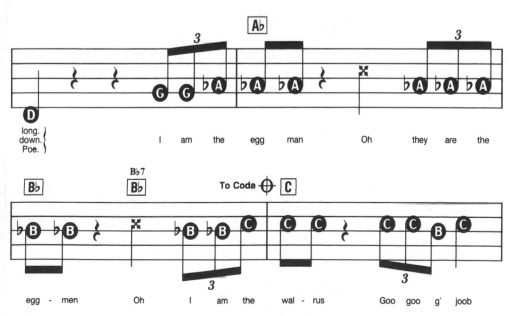

long.
down.
Poe.

I am the egg man Oh they are the

egg - men Oh I am the wal - rus Goo goo g' joob

Mis - ter cit - y p'lice - man sit - ting pret - ty lit - tle p'lice - men in a

row_____ See how they fly like Lu - cy in the sky see

how_____ they run I'm cry - ing I'm cry -

- ing I'm cry - ing I'm cry -

ing

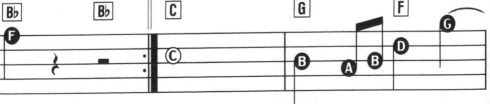

(Instrumental)

81

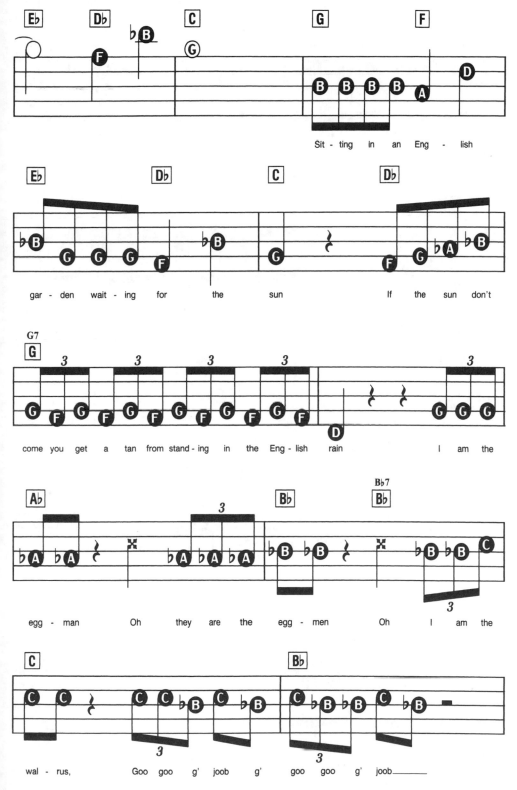

82

Ex - pert tex - pert chok - ing smok - ers don't you think the jok - er laughs at

you?_____ See how they smile like pigs in a sty, see

D.S. al Coda
(Return to 𝄋
and Play to ⊕
and skip to Coda)

how_____ they hide I'm cry - ing.

CODA

wal - rus. Goo goo g' joob g' goo goo g' joob_____

Repeat and Fade

Goo goo g' goo g' goo goo g' joob joob *(Juba juba juba)*

I'm Looking Through You

Registration 2
Rhythm: Rock

Words and Music by John Lennon
and Paul McCartney

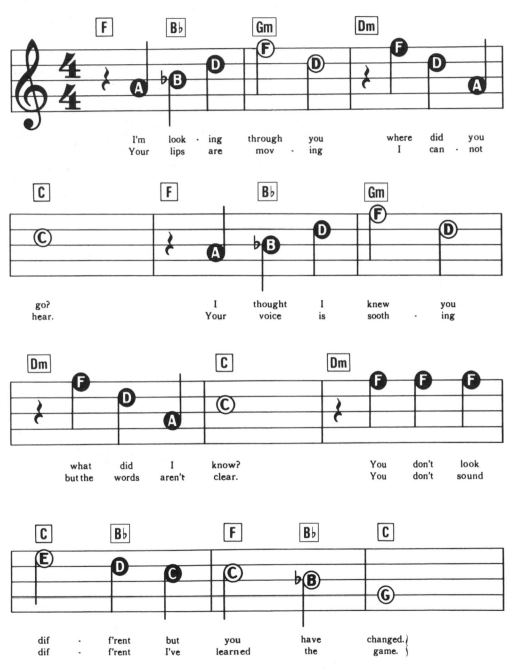

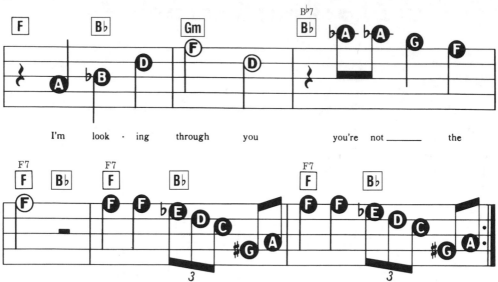

I'm look · ing through you you're not _____ the

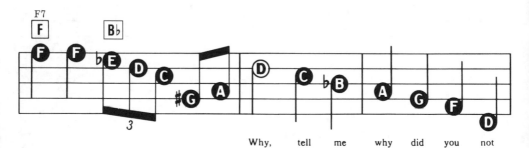

same.

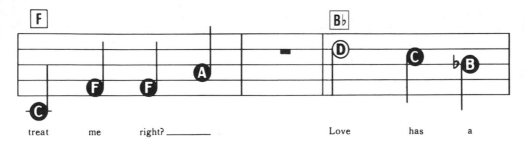

Why, tell me why did you not

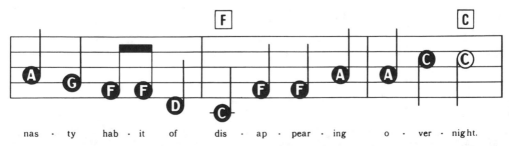

treat me right? _____ Love has a

nas · ty hab · it of dis · ap · pear · ing o · ver · night.

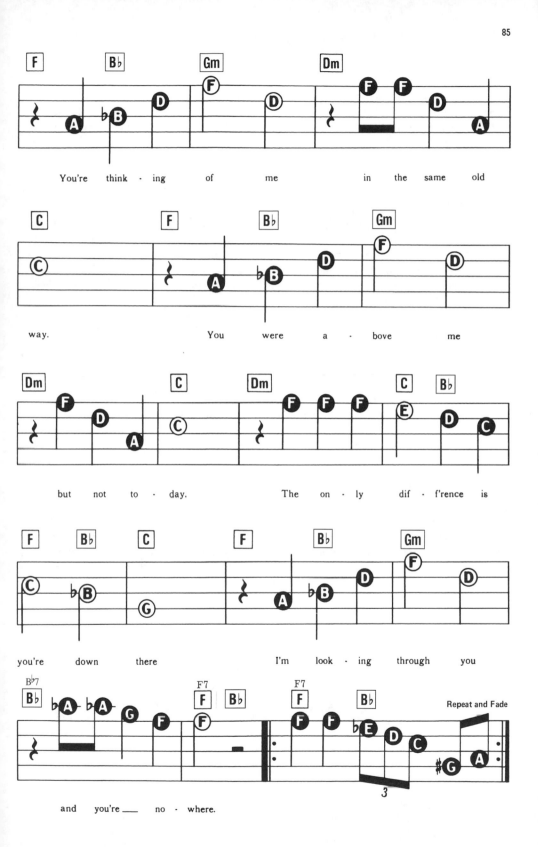

I Feel Fine

Registration 9
Rhythm: Rock or Jazz Rock

Words and Music by John Lennon
and Paul McCartney

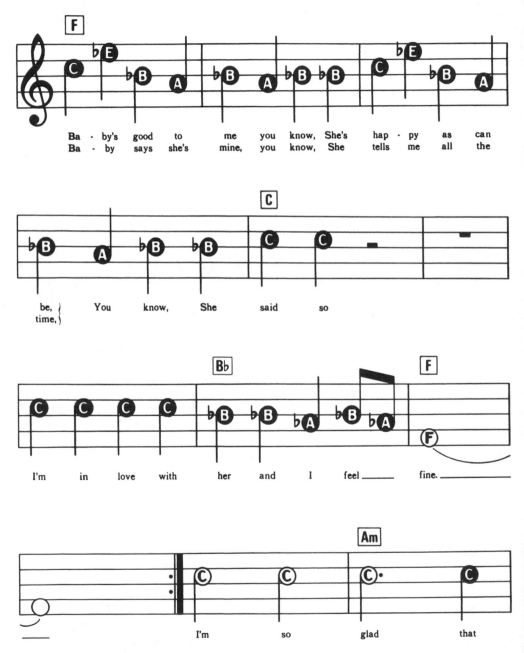

Ba - by's good to me you know, She's hap - py as can
Ba - by says she's mine, you know, She tells me all the

be, } You know, She said so
time, }

I'm in love with her and I feel _____ fine. _____

_____ I'm so glad that

87

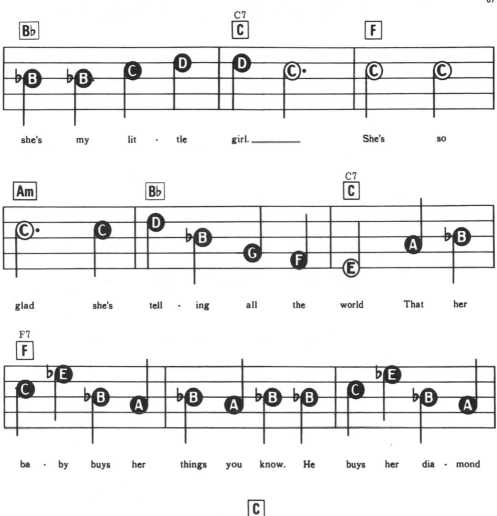

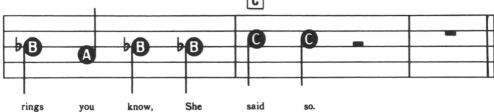

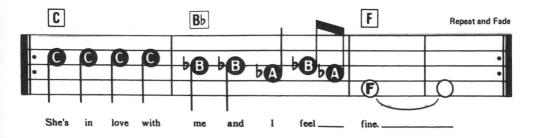

I Saw Her Standing There

Registration 2
Rhythm: Rock

Words and Music by John Lennon
and Paul McCartney

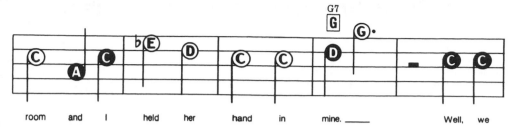

room and I held her hand in mine. _____ Well, we

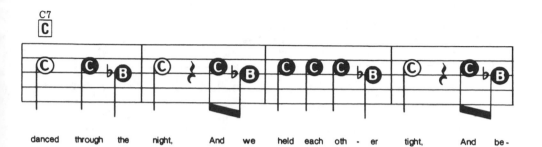

danced through the night, And we held each oth - er tight, And be -

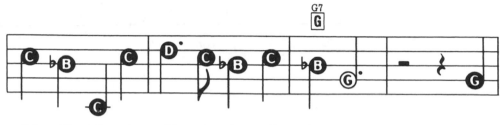

fore too long, I fell in love with her. _____ Now

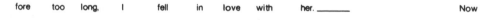

I'll nev - er dance with an - oth - er, Oh, since I

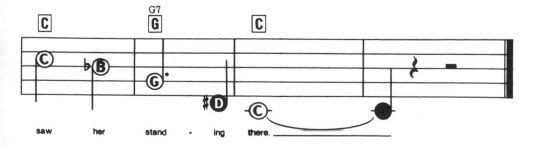

saw her stand - ing there. _____

I Should Have Known Better

Registration 3
Rhythm: Rock

Words and Music by John Lennon
and Paul McCartney

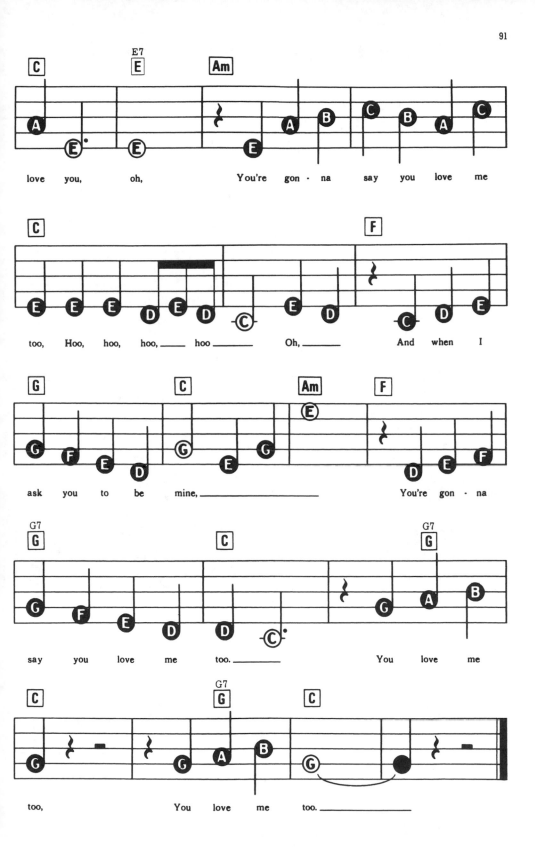

I Want to Hold Your Hand

Registration 3
Rhythm: Rock

Words and Music by John Lennon
and Paul McCartney

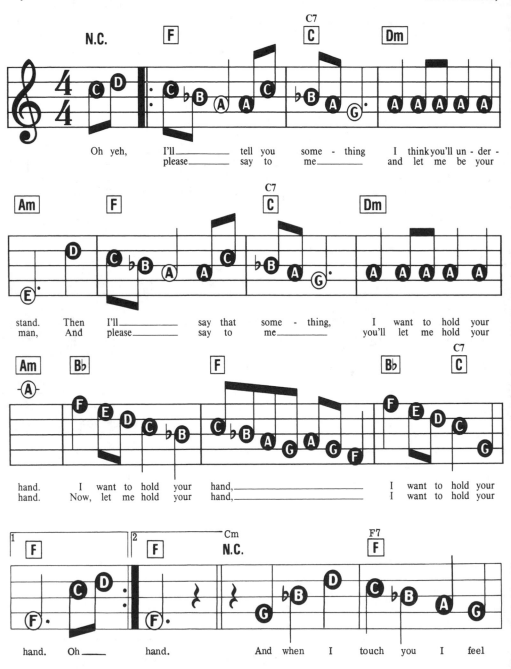

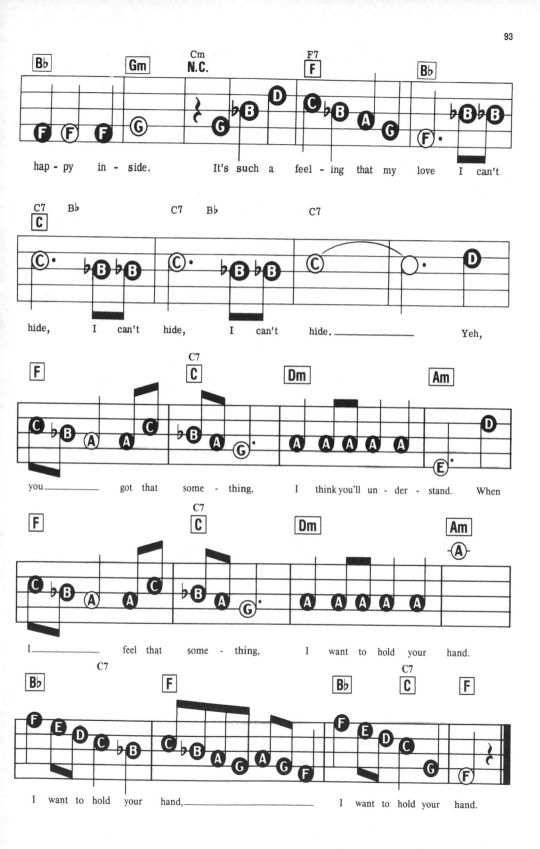

I Want to Tell You

Registration 4
Rhythm: Rock

Words and Music by
George Harrison

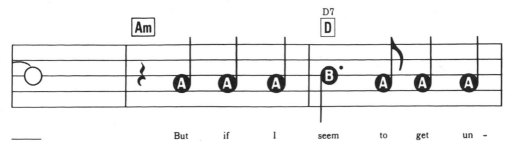

But if I seem to get un –

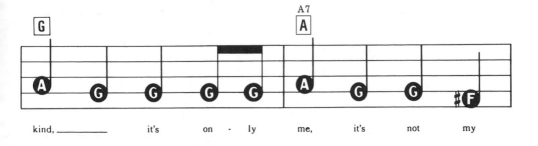

kind, _____ it's on - ly me, it's not my

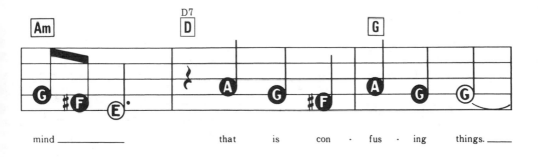

mind _____ that is con · fus · ing things. ____

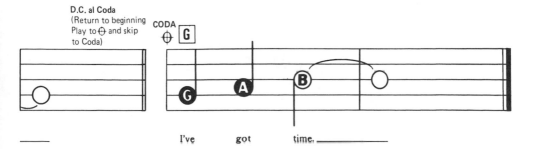

I've got time. _____

I Will

Registration 4
Rhythm: Rock or Slow Rock

Words and Music by John Lennon
and Paul McCartney

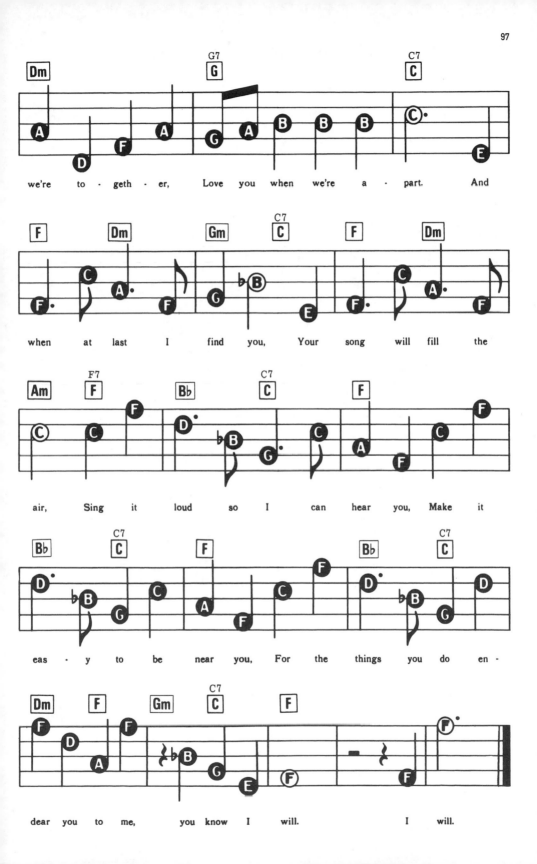

I'll Follow the Sun

Registration 9
Rhythm: Rock or Latin

Words and Music by John Lennon
and Paul McCartney

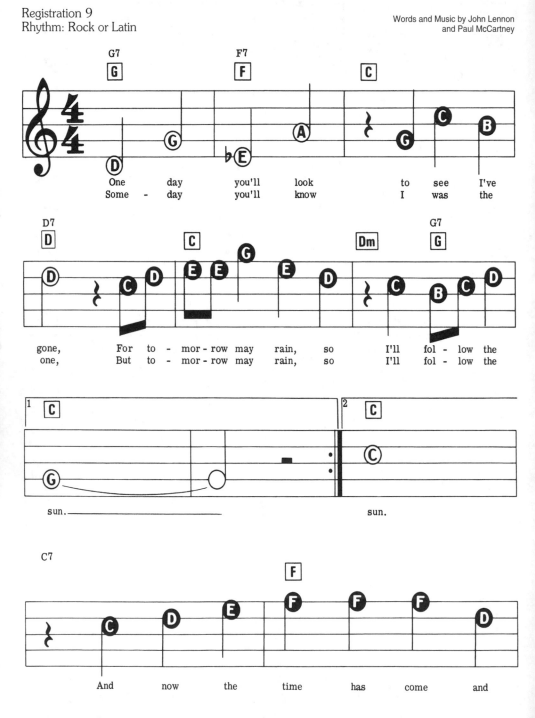

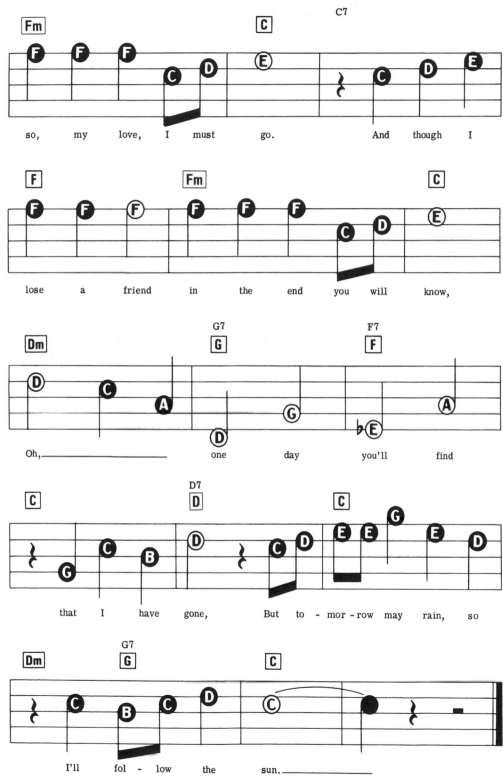

I've Just Seen a Face

Registration 4
Rhythm: Rock

Words and Music by John Lennon
and Paul McCartney

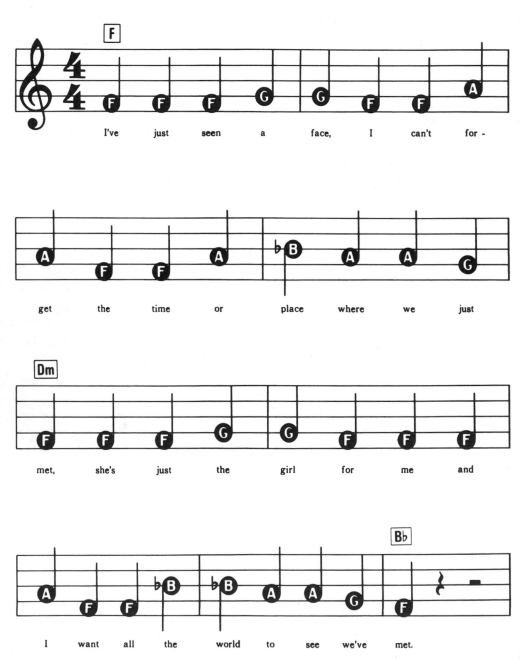

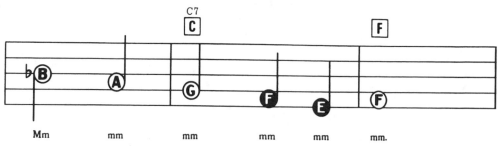

Mm mm mm mm mm mm.

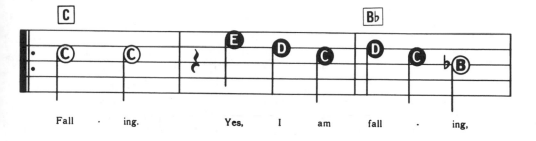

Fall · ing. Yes, I am fall · ing,

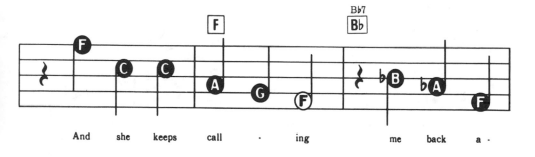

And she keeps call · ing me back a -

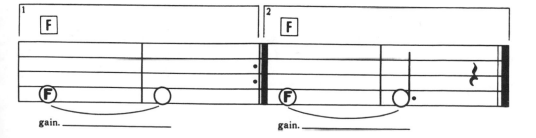

gain. _____ gain. _____

If I Fell

Registration 9
Rhythm: Rock or Latin

Words and Music by John Lennon
and Paul McCartney

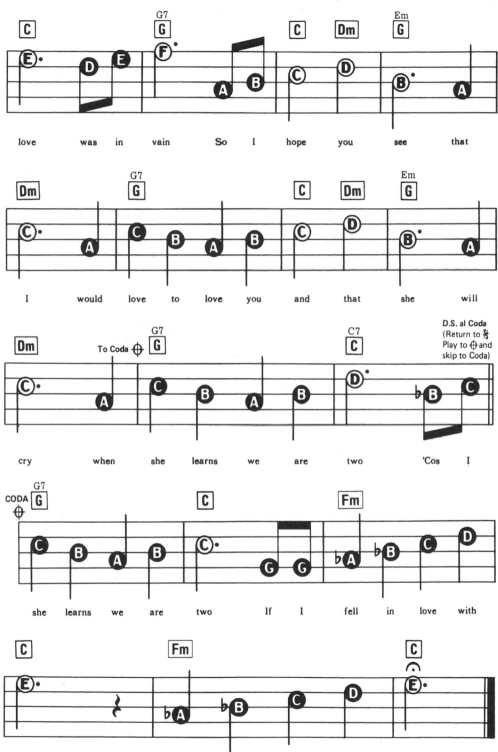

If I Needed Someone

Registration 8
Rhythm: 8 Beat

Words and Music by
George Harrison

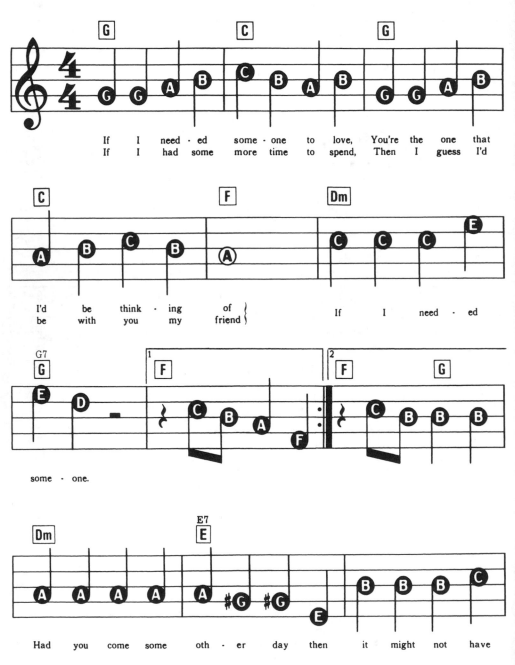

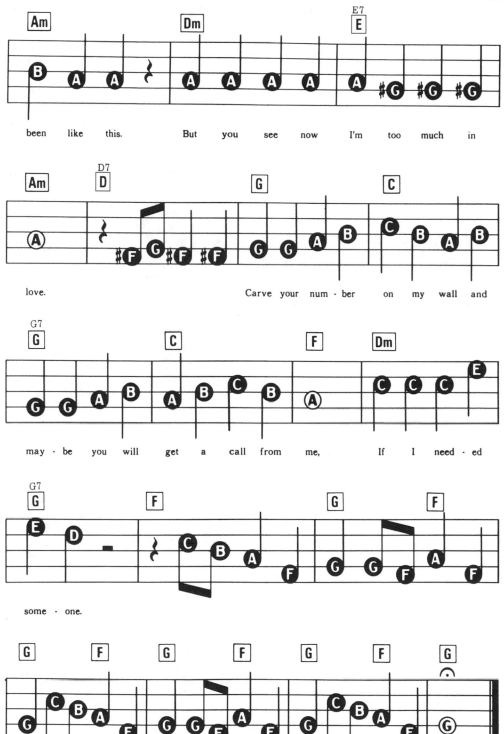

been like this. But you see now I'm too much in love. Carve your num·ber on my wall and may·be you will get a call from me, If I need·ed some·one.

In My Life

Registration 2
Rhythm: Rock or Jazz Rock

Words and Music by John Lennon
and Paul McCartney

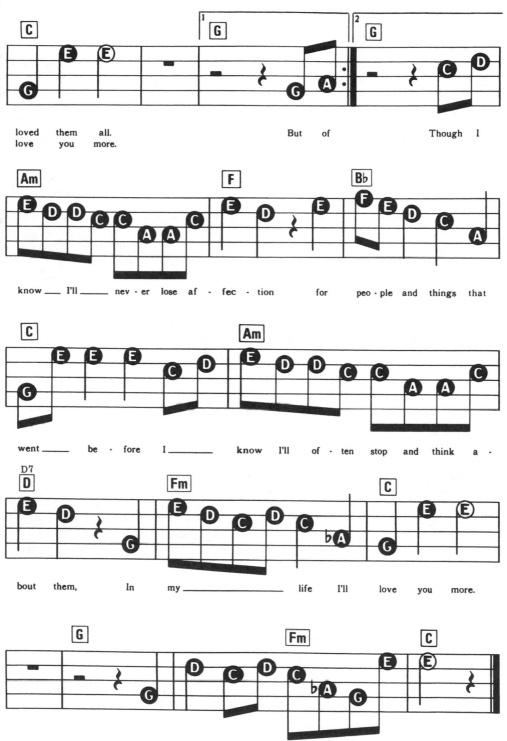

Julia

Registration 9
Rhythm: Rock

Words and Music by John Lennon
and Paul McCartney

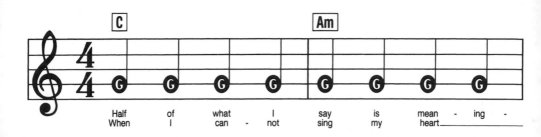

Half   of   what   I   say   is   mean - ing -
When   I   can -   not   sing   my   heart_____

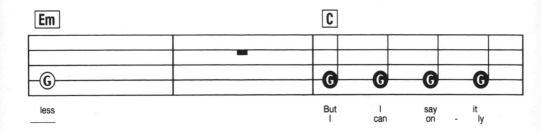

less   But   I   say   it
_____   I   can   on -   ly

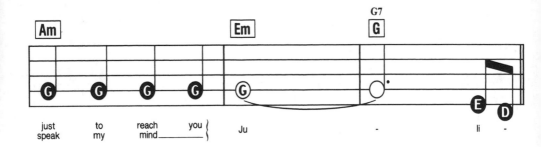

just   to   reach   you }   Ju   li -
speak   my   mind_____

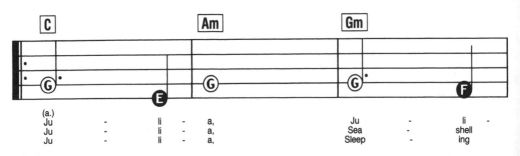

(a.)
Ju   -   li -   a,   Ju   -   li -
Ju   -   li -   a,   Sea   -   shell
Ju   -   li -   a,   Sleep   -   ing

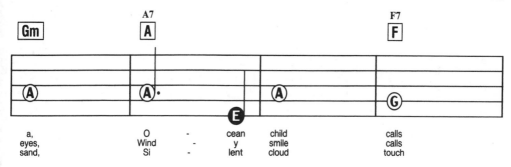

a,   O - cean   child   calls
eyes,   Wind - y   smile   calls
sand,   Si - lent   cloud   touch

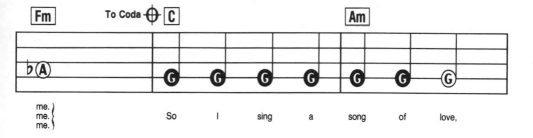

me.
me.
me.

So   I   sing   a   song   of   love,

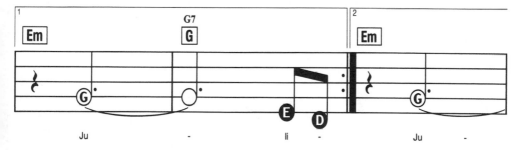

Ju - li - Ju -

- li - a.   Her   hair   of

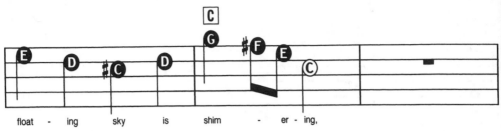

float - ing sky is shim - er - ing,

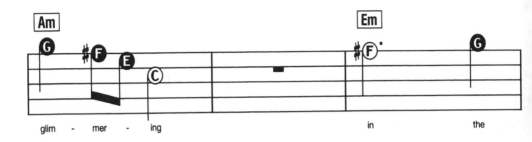

glim - mer - ing in the

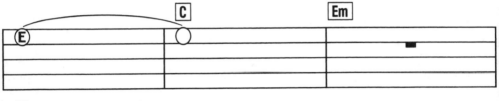

sun._____

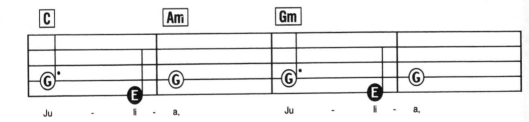

Ju - li - a, Ju - li - a,

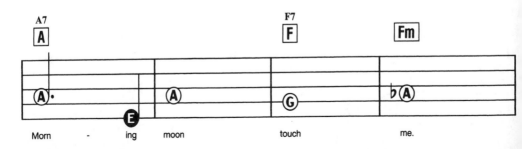

Morn - ing moon touch me.

111

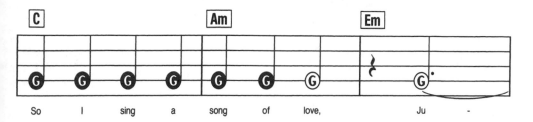

So I sing a song of love, Ju -

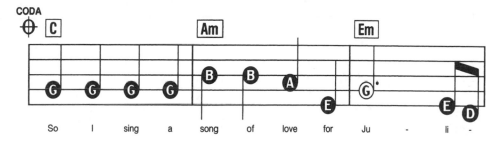

D.C. al Coda
(Return to beginning
Play to ⊕ and
skip to Coda)

- li - a.

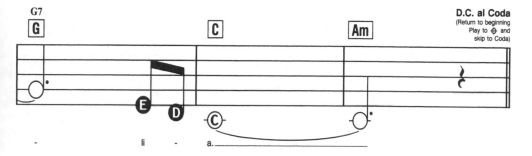

So I sing a song of love for Ju - li -

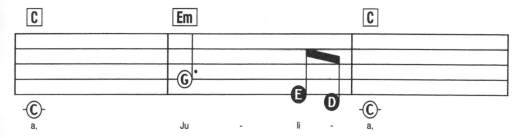

a, Ju - li - a,

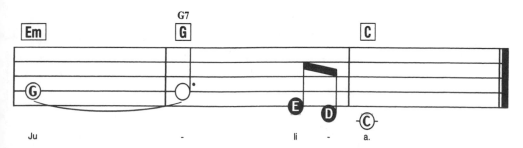

Ju - li - a.

Lady Madonna

Registration 4
Rhythm: Rock

Words and Music by John Lennon
and Paul McCartney

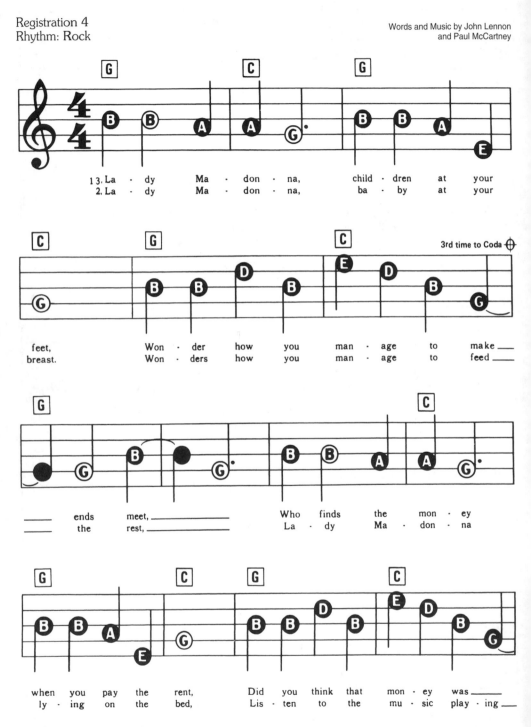

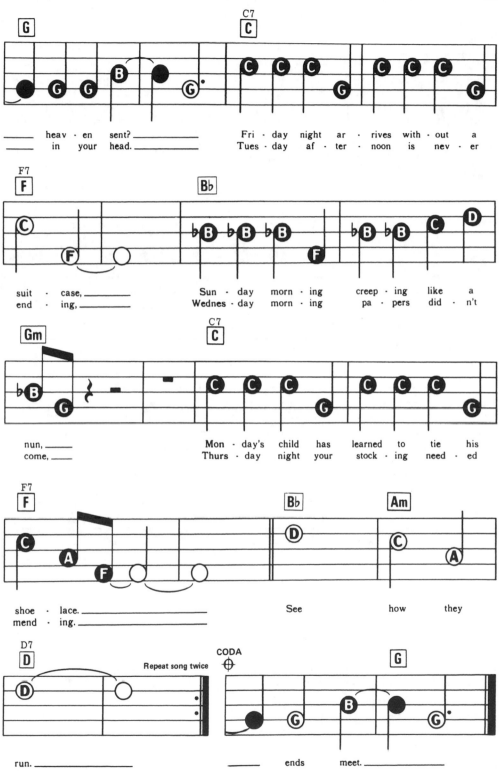

heav · en sent? _____ Fri · day night ar · rives with · out a

in your head. _____ Tues · day af · ter · noon is nev · er

suit · case, _____ Sun · day morn · ing creep · ing like a

end · ing, _____ Wednes · day morn · ing pa · pers did · n't

nun, _____ Mon · day's child has learned to tie his

come, _____ Thurs · day night your stock · ing need · ed

shoe · lace. _____ See how they

mend · ing. _____

run. _____ _____ ends meet. _____

Let It Be

Registration 3
Rhythm: Rock

Words and Music by John Lennon
and Paul McCartney

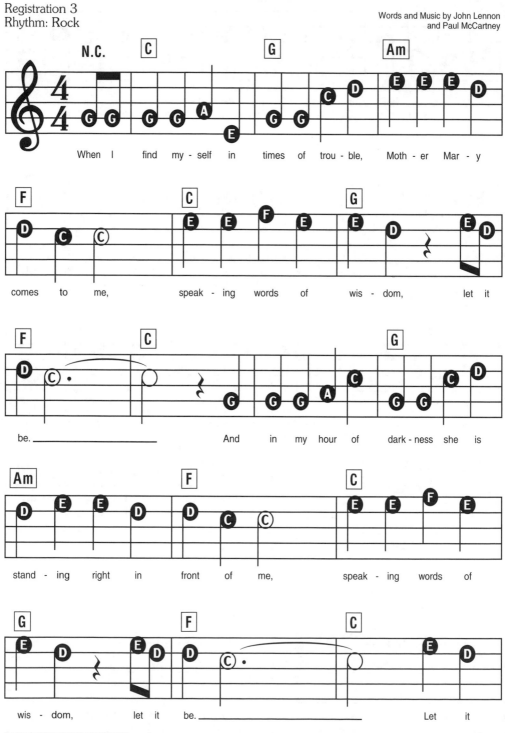

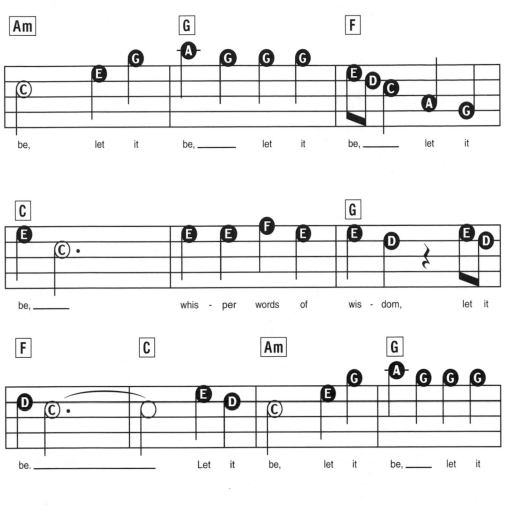

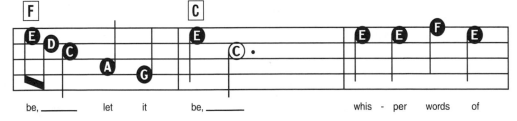

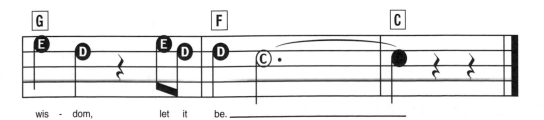

The Long and Winding Road

Registration 1
Rhythm: Ballad

Words and Music by John Lennon
and Paul McCartney

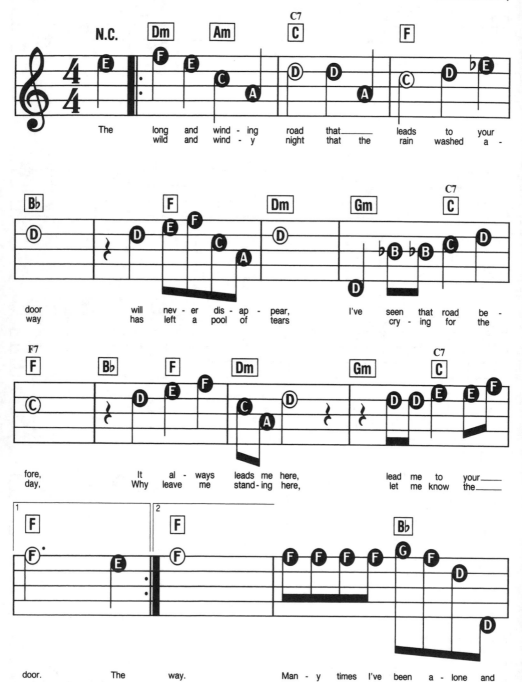

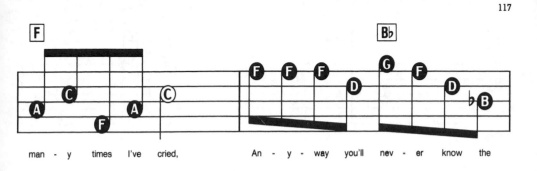

many - y times I've cried, An - y - way you'll nev - er know the

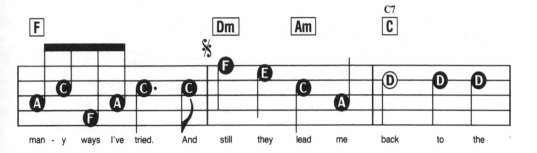

many - y ways I've tried. And still they lead me back to the

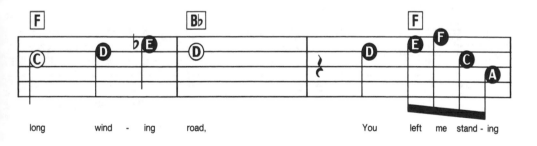

long wind - ing road, You left me stand - ing

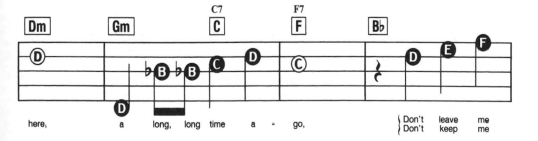

here, a long, long time a - go, Don't leave me
Don't keep me

118

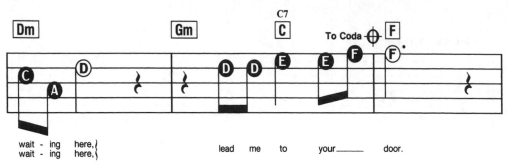

wait - ing here,
wait - ing here,   lead   me   to   your___   door.

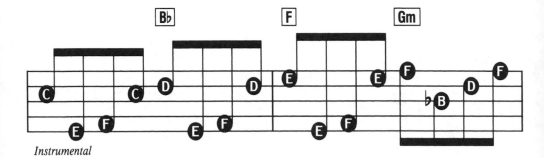

Instrumental

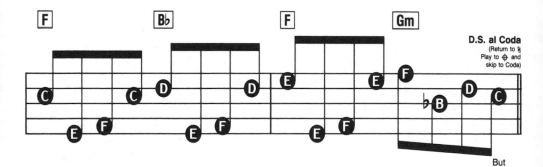

D.S. al Coda
(Return to %
Play to ⊕ and
skip to Coda)

But

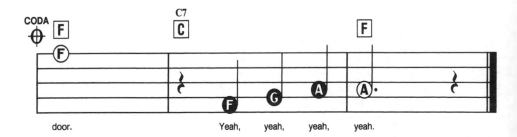

door.   Yeah,   yeah,   yeah,   yeah.

Martha My Dear

Registration 8
Rhythm: Swing or Shuffle

Words and Music by John Lennon
and Paul McCartney

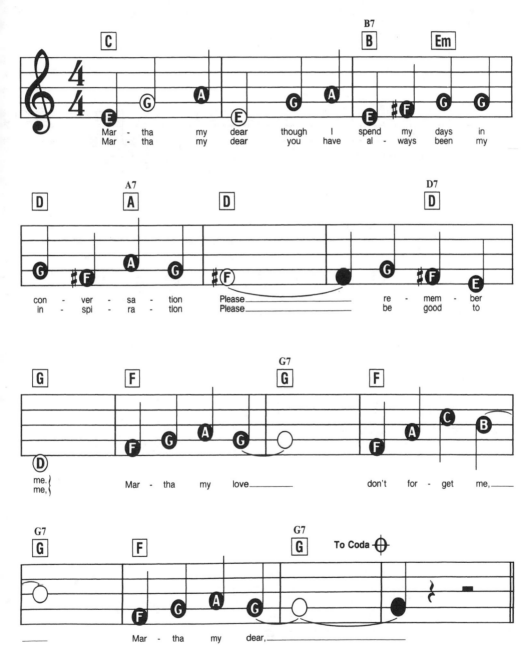

120

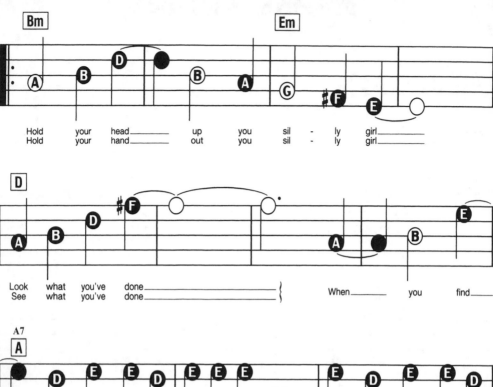

Hold your head_____ up you sil - ly girl_____
Hold your hand_____ out you sil - ly girl_____

Look what you've done_____ When_____ you find_____
See what you've done_____

A7

_____ your - self in the thick of it   Help your - self to a

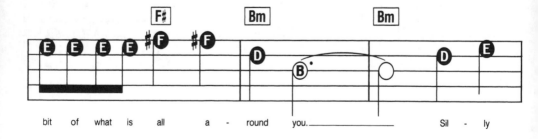

bit of what is all a - round you._____ Sil - ly

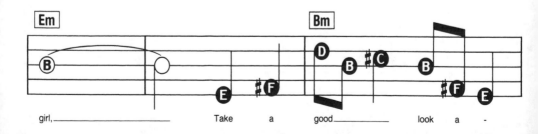

girl,_____ Take a good_____ look a -

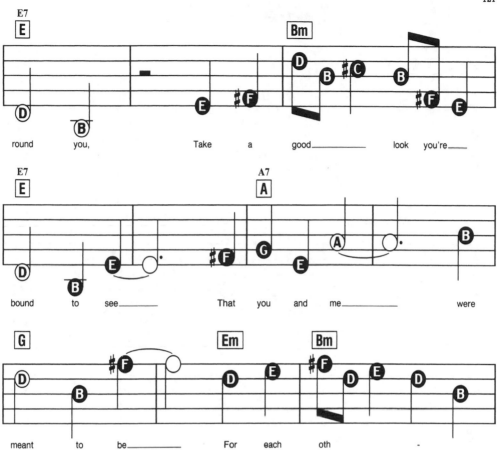

round you,   you,   Take   a   good_____   look   you're____

bound   to   see_____   That   you   and   me_____   were

meant   to   be_____   For   each   oth   -

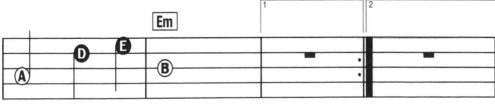

er   sil - ly   girl.

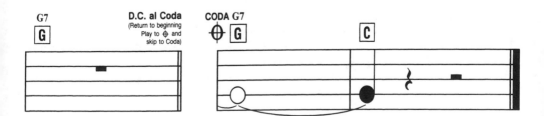

Love Me Do

Registration 8
Rhythm: Country Swing

Words and Music by John Lennon
and Paul McCartney

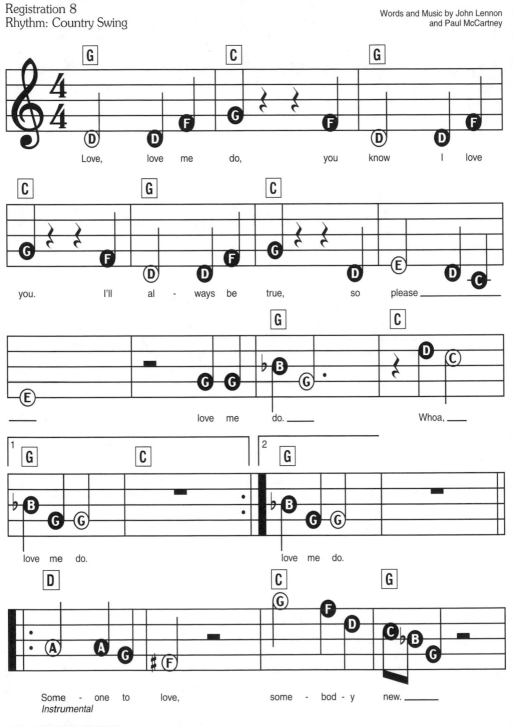

123

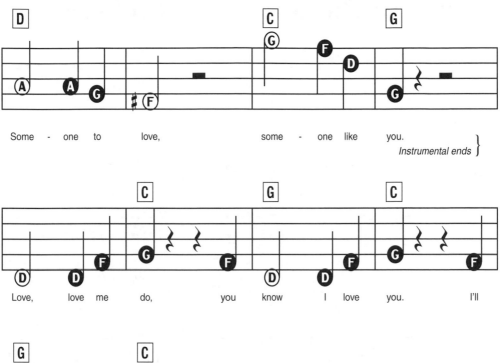

Some - one to love, some - one like you.

Instrumental ends

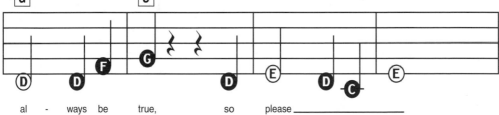

Love, love me do, you know I love you. I'll

al - ways be true, so please ____

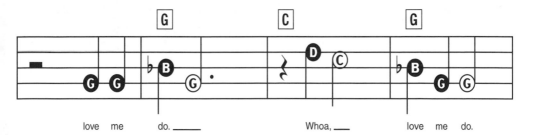

love me do. ____ Whoa, ___ love me do.

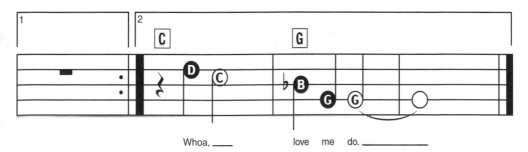

Whoa, ___ love me do. ____

Lucy in the Sky with Diamonds

Registration 8
Rhythm: Waltz

Words and Music by John Lennon
and Paul McCartney

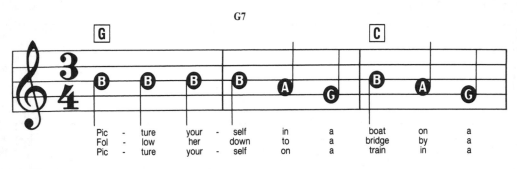

Pic - ture your - self	in a	boat on a
Fol - low her down	to a	bridge by a
Pic - ture your - self	on a	train in a

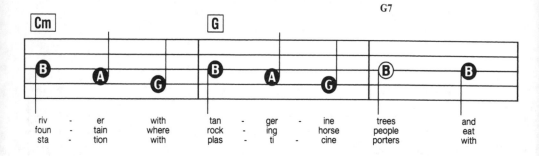

riv - er	with	tan - ger - ine	trees and
foun - tain	where	rock - ing horse	people eat
sta - tion	with	plas - ti - cine	porters with

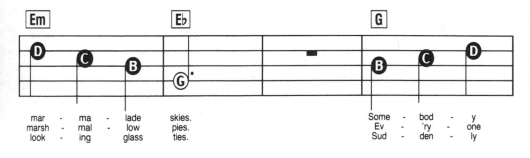

mar - ma - lade skies.	Some - bod - y
marsh - mal - low pies.	Ev - 'ry - one
look - ing glass ties.	Sud - den - ly

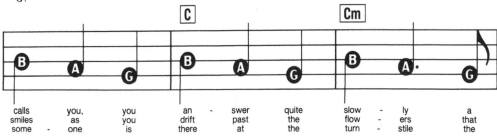

calls you, you	an - swer quite	slow - ly a
smiles as you	drift past the	flow - ers that
some - one is	there at the	turn - stile the

125

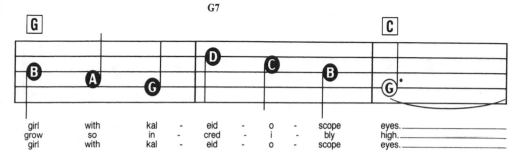

girl with kal - eid - o - scope eyes.
grow so in - cred - i - bly high.
girl with kal - eid - o - scope eyes.

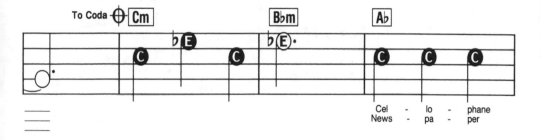

Cel - lo - phane
News - pa - per

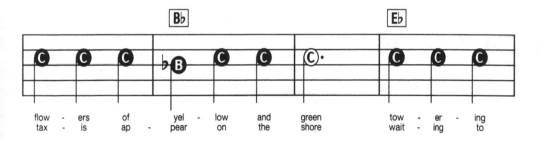

flow - ers of yel - low and green tow - er - ing
tax - is ap - pear on the shore wait - ing to

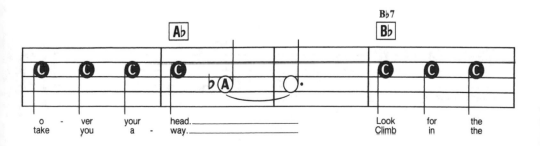

o - ver your head.
take you a - way.

Look for the
Climb in the

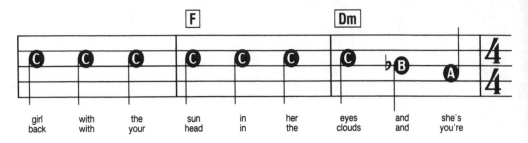

girl with the sun in her eyes and she's
back with your head in the clouds and you're

Rhythm: Rock

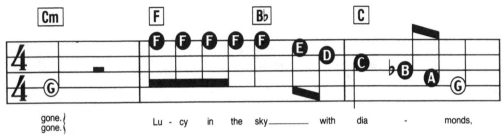

gone. Lu - cy in the sky_____ with dia - monds,
gone.

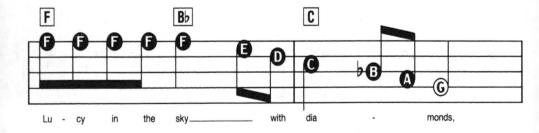

Lu - cy in the sky_____ with dia - monds,

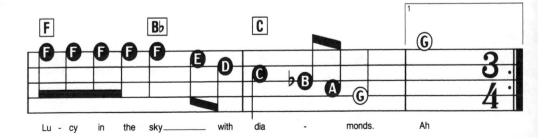

Lu - cy in the sky_____ with dia - monds. Ah

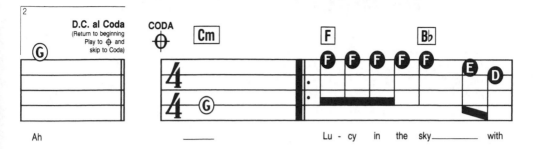

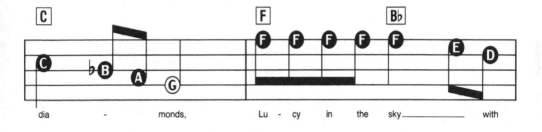

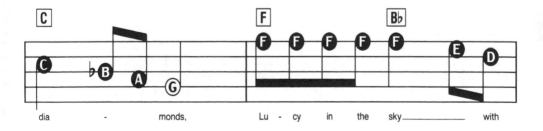

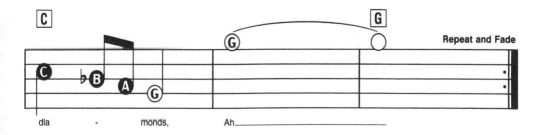

Magical Mystery Tour

Registration 2
Rhythm: Rock

Words and Music by John Lennon
and Paul McCartney

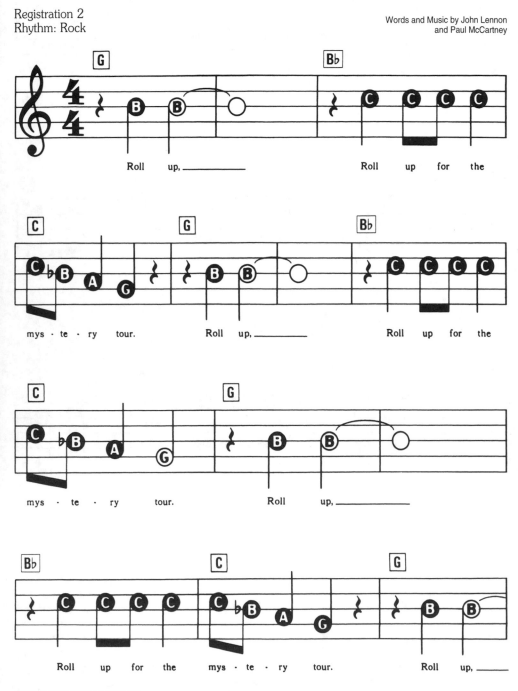

129

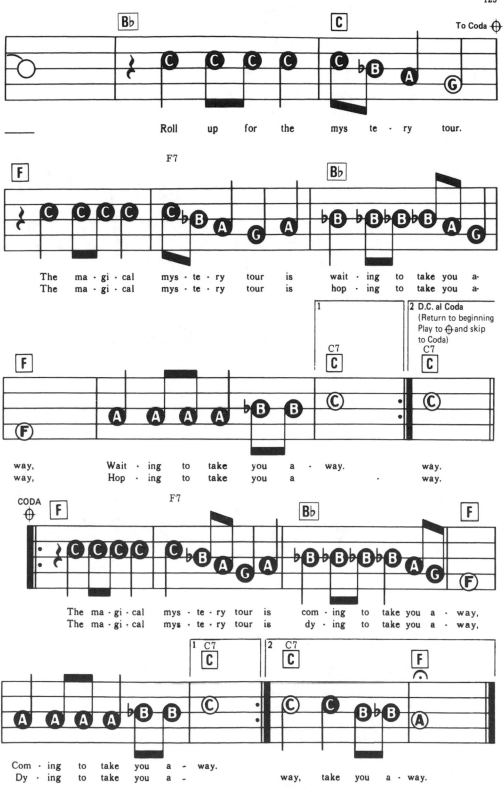

Michelle

Registration 1
Rhythm: Rock

Words and Music by John Lennon
and Paul McCartney

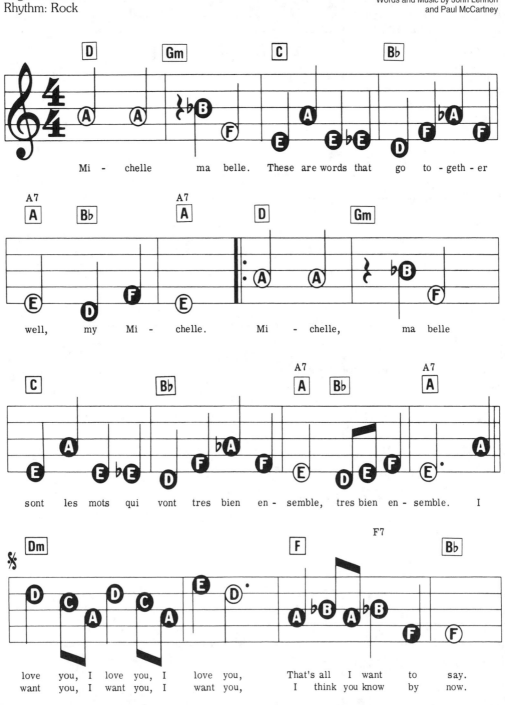

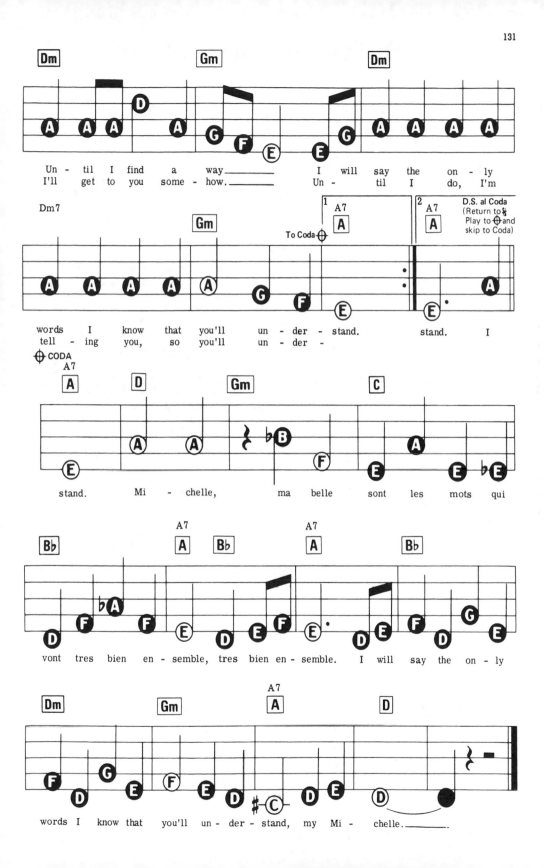

Mother Nature's Son

Registration 4
Rhythm: 8 Beat or Rock

Words and Music by John Lennon
and Paul McCartney

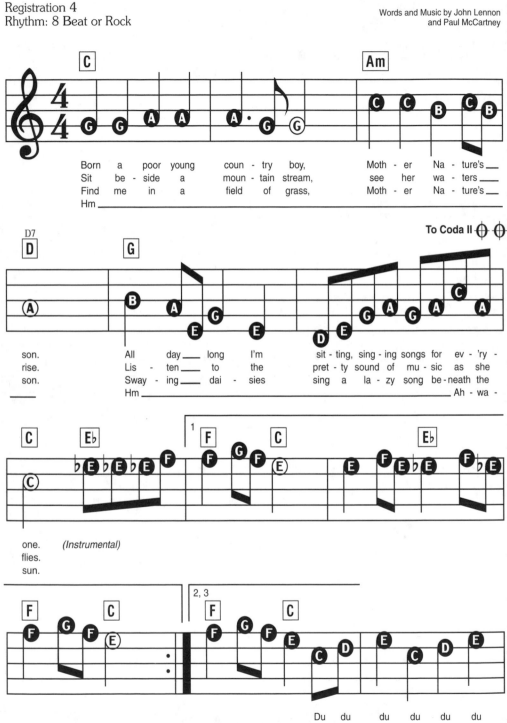

133

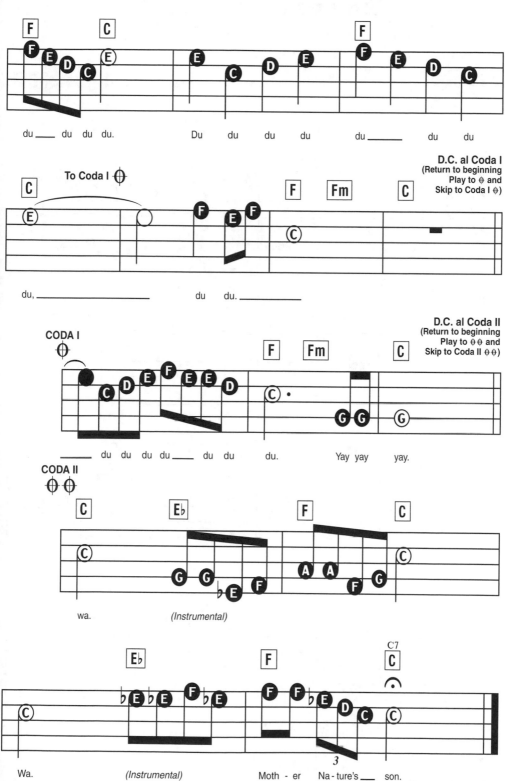

Norwegian Wood
(This Bird Has Flown)

Registration 8
Rhythm: Waltz

Words and Music by John Lennon
and Paul McCartney

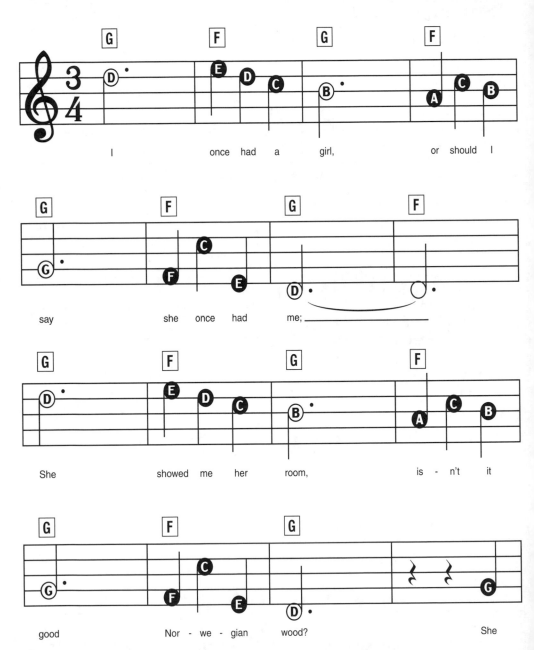

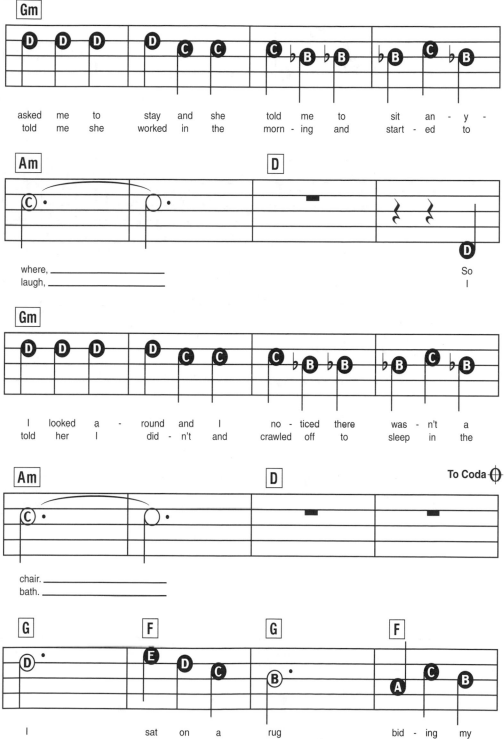

%

Gm

asked me to stay and she told me to sit an - y -
told me she worked in the morn - ing and start - ed to

Am   **D**

where, _____   So
laugh, _____   I

Gm

I looked a - round and I no - ticed there was - n't a
told her I did - n't and crawled off to sleep in the

Am   **D**   **To Coda** ⊕

chair. _____
bath. _____

G   **F**   **G**   **F**

I   sat on a rug   bid - ing my

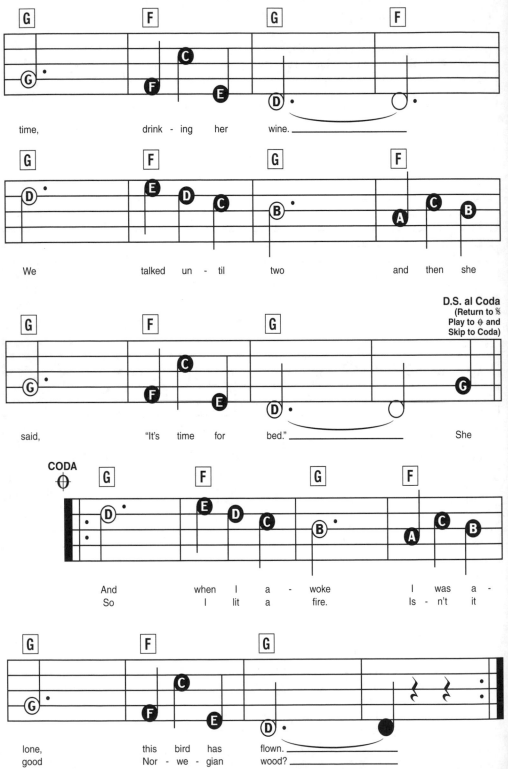

She Loves You

Registration 1
Rhythm: Rock

Words and Music by John Lennon
and Paul McCartney

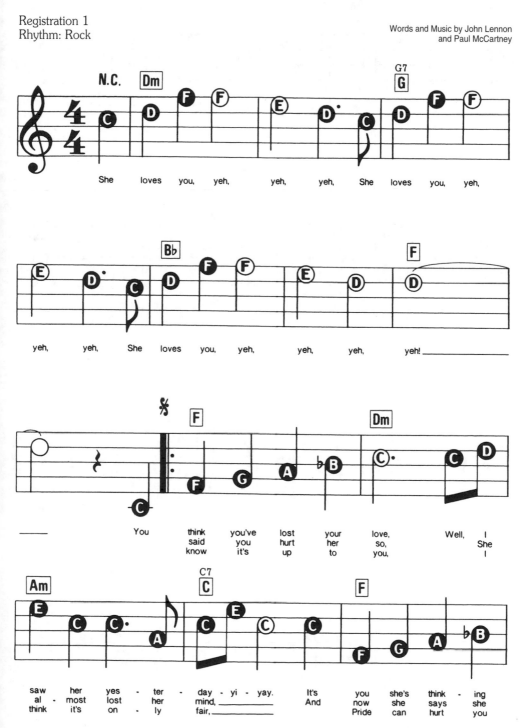

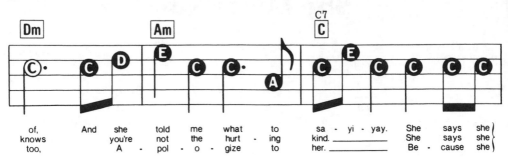

of,   And   she   told   me   what   to   sa - yi - yay.   She   says   she
knows   you're not   the   hurt - ing   kind. _____   She   says   she
too,   A - pol - o - gize   to   her. _____   Be - cause   she

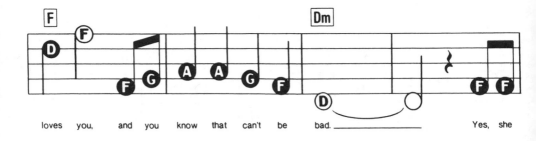

loves   you,   and   you   know   that   can't   be   bad. _____   Yes,   she

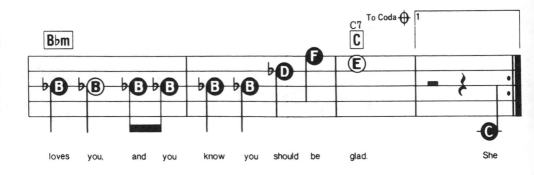

loves   you,   and   you   know   you   should   be   glad.   She

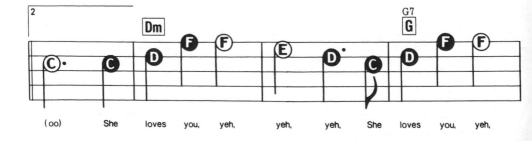

(oo)   She   loves   you,   yeh,   yeh,   yeh,   She   loves   you,   yeh,

123

yeh, yeh, And with a love like that you know you should be

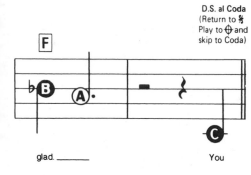

D.S. al Coda
(Return to 𝄋
Play to ⊕ and
skip to Coda)

⊕ CODA

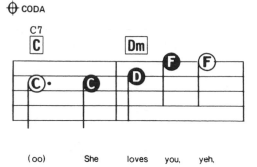

glad. _____ You (oo) She loves you, yeh,

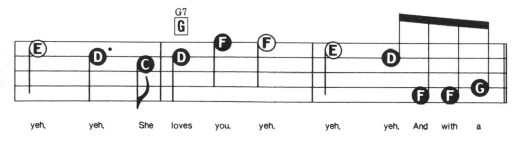

yeh, yeh, She loves you, yeh, yeh, yeh, And with a

Repeat and Fade

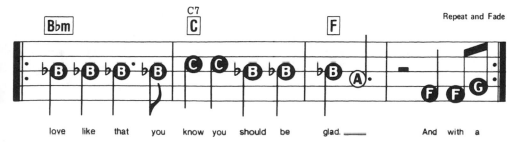

love like that you know you should be glad. _____ And with a

Nowhere Man

Registration 2
Rhythm: Rock

Words and Music by John Lennon
and Paul McCartney

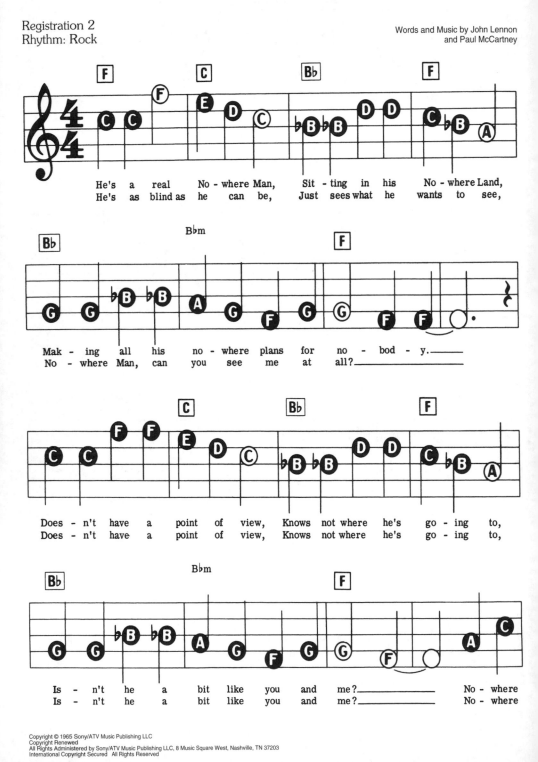

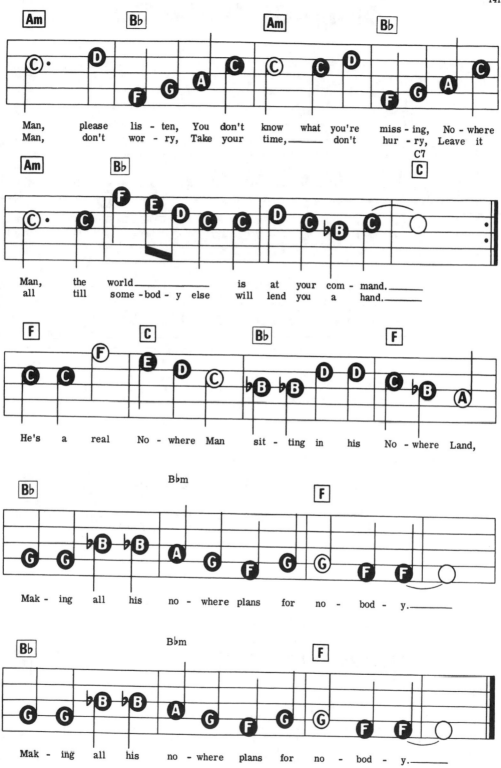

Ob-La-Di, Ob-La-Da

Registration 9
Rhythm: Rock

Words and Music by John Lennon
and Paul McCartney

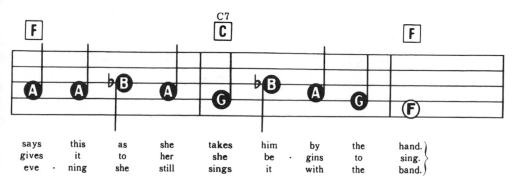

says this as she takes him by the hand.
gives it to her she begins to sing.
eve - ning she her still sings it with the band.

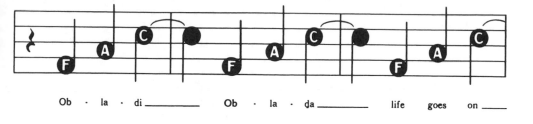

Ob - la - di _____ Ob - la - da _____ life goes on _____

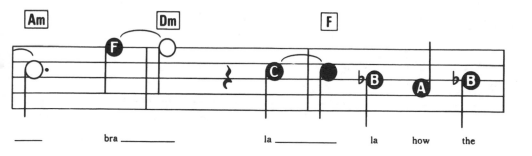

_____ bra _____ la _____ la how the

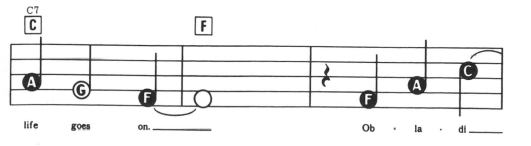

life goes on. _____ Ob - la - di _____

144

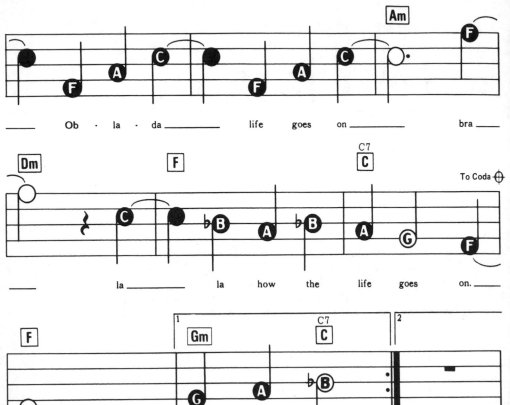

Ob · la · da ___ life goes on ___ bra ___

la ___ la how the life goes on. ___

In a cou · ple of years they have built a home ___

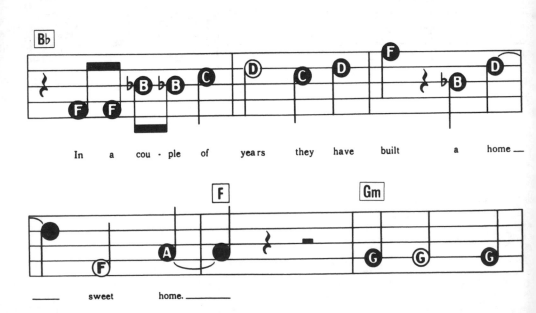

sweet home. ___

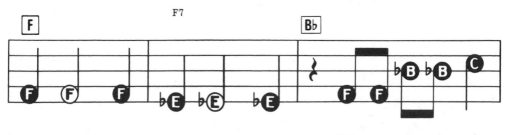

F7

With a cou‑ple of

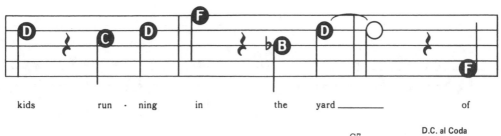

kids run‑ning in the yard_____ of

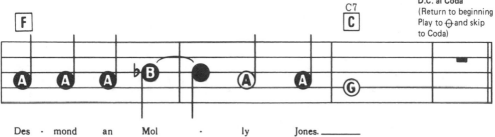

Des‑mond an Mol‑ly Jones._____

D.C. al Coda
(Return to beginning
Play to ⊕ and skip
to Coda)

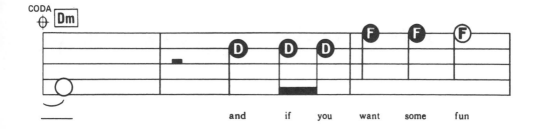

CODA

_____ and if you want some fun

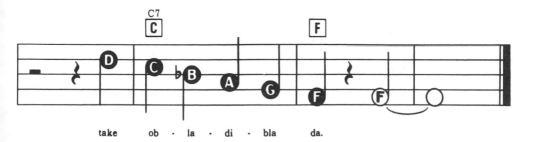

take ob‑la‑di‑bla‑da.

Paperback Writer

Registration 4
Rhythm: Rock

Words and Music by John Lennon
and Paul McCartney

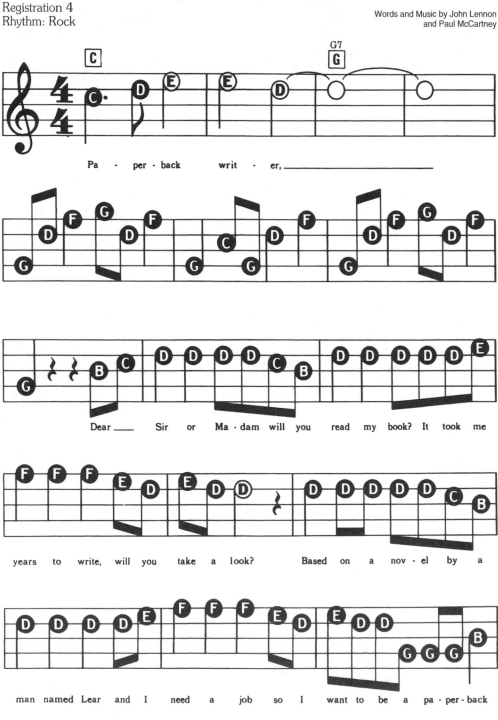

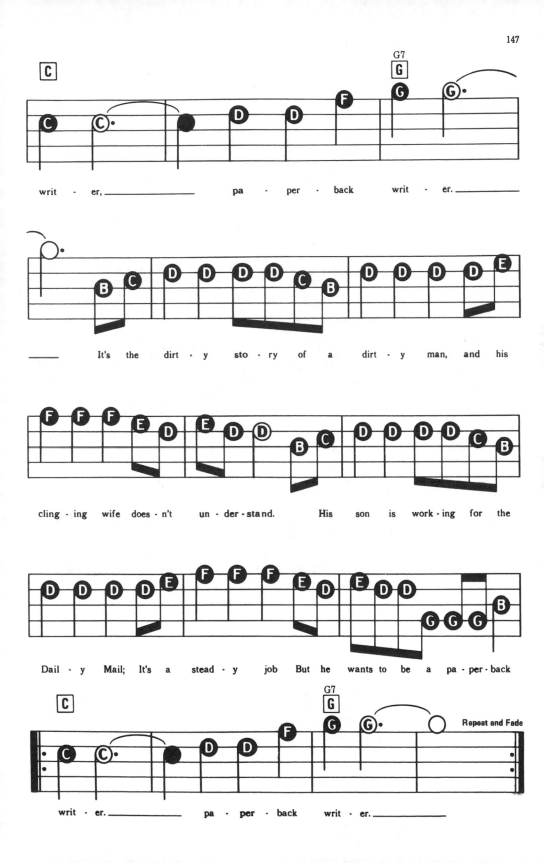

writ - er,_____ pa - per - back writ - er._____

_____ It's the dirt - y sto - ry of a dirt - y man, and his

cling - ing wife does - n't un - der - sta nd. His son is work - ing for the

Dail - y Mail; It's a stead - y job But he wants to be a pa - per - back

writ - er._____ pa - per - back writ - er._____

Penny Lane

Registration 2
Rhythm: Rock

Words and Music by John Lennon
and Paul McCartney

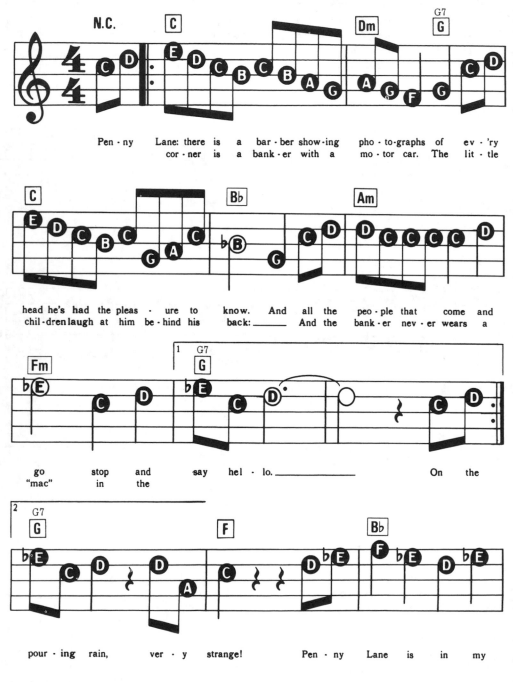

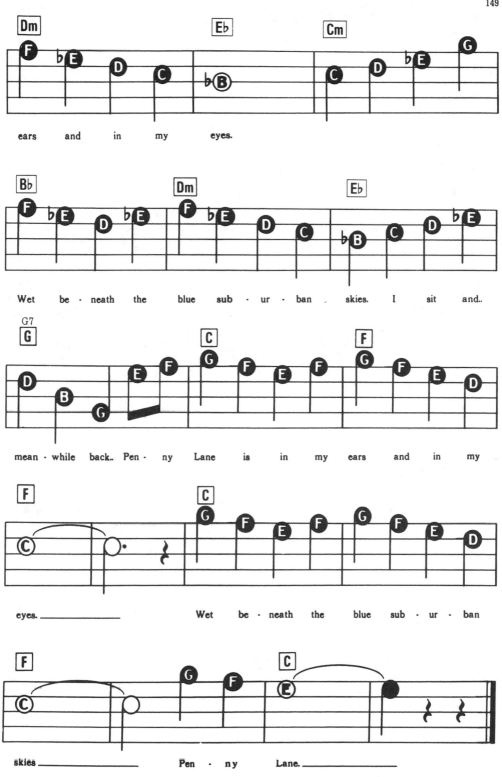

Please Please Me

Registration 8
Rhythm: Rock

Words and Music by John Lennon
and Paul McCartney

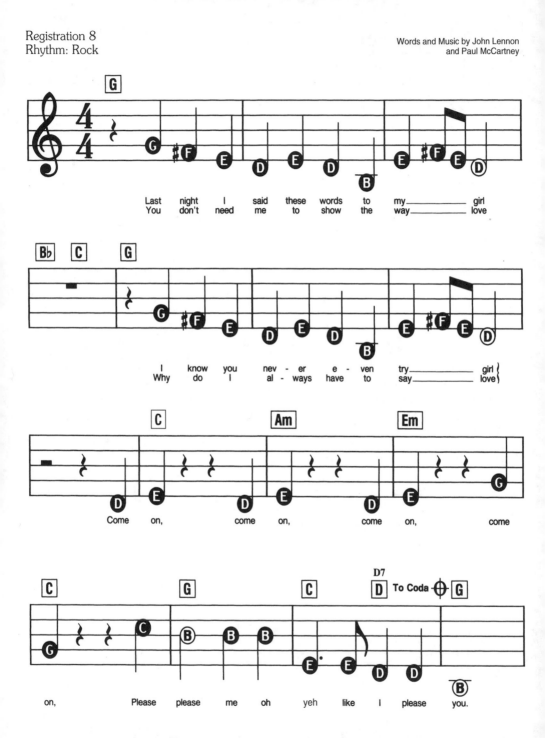

Last night I said these words to my_____ girl
You don't need me to show the way_____ love

I know you nev - er e - ven try_____ girl
Why do I al - ways have to say_____ love

Come on, come on, come on, come

on, Please please me oh yeh like I please you.

151

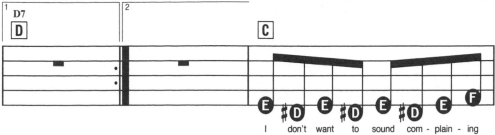

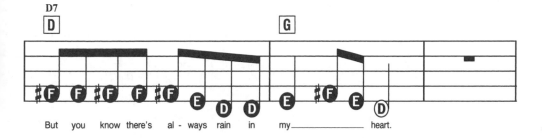

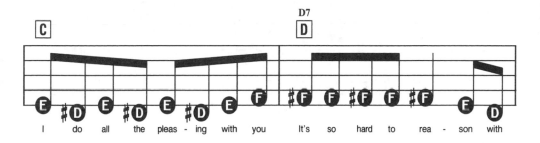

D.C. (lyric 1) al Coda
(Return to beginning
Play to ⊕ and skip to Coda)

CODA
⊕ G

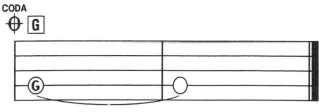

Rocky Raccoon

Registration 5
Rhythm: Fox Trot or Swing

Words and Music by John Lennon
and Paul McCartney

Rock · y   Rac · coon _____   checked   in · to   his   room _____
She   and   her   man _____   who   called   him · self   Dan _____   were

on · ly   to   find _____   Gid · eon's   Bi ·   ble. _____
in   the   next   room _____   at   the   hoe ·   down. _____

Rock · y   had   come _____   e · quipped   with   a   gun _____   to
Rock · y   burst   in _____   and   grin · ning   a   grin, _____   He said,

shoot   off   the   legs _____   of   his   ri ·   val. _____
"Dan · ny   boy,   this _____   is   a   show ·   down."

Run for Your Life

Registration 3
Rhythm: Rock

Words and Music by John Lennon
and Paul McCartney

Well I'd rath - er see you dead lit - tle girl than to
know that I'm a wick - ed guy and I was

be with an - oth - er man You'd bet - ter keep your
born with a jeal - ous mind And I can't spend my

head lit - tle girl or I won't know where I am
whole life tryin' just to make you toe the line

You'd bet - ter
run for your life if you can lit - tle girl ____ Hide your head in the

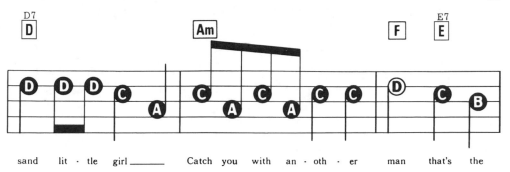

sand   lit · tle   girl _____   Catch you with an · oth · er   man   that's   the

end   a   lit · tle   gir l.

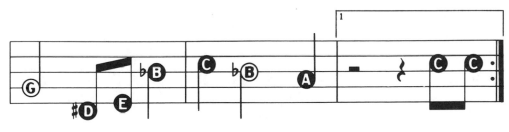

Well   you

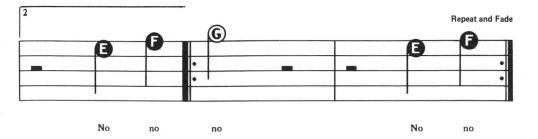

No   no   no   No   no

Sgt. Pepper's Lonely Hearts Club Band

Registration 4
Rhythm: Rock

Words and Music by John Lennon
and Paul McCartney

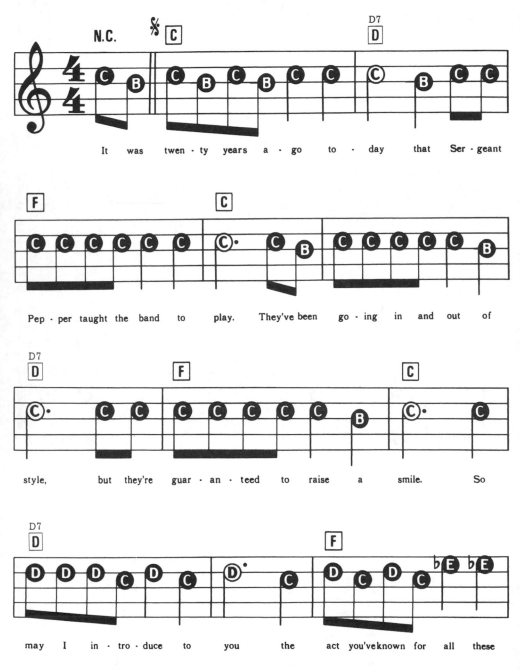

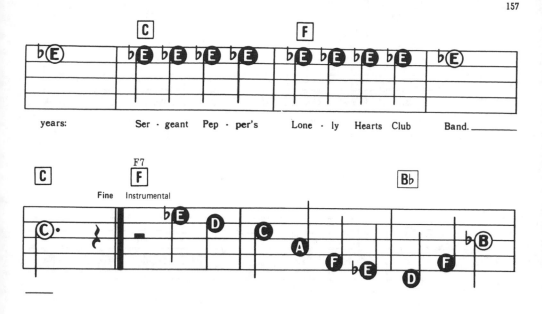

years: Ser · geant Pep · per's Lone · ly Hearts Club Band. _____

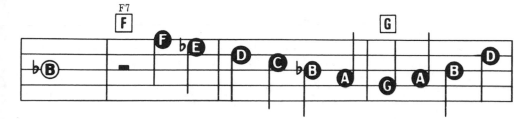

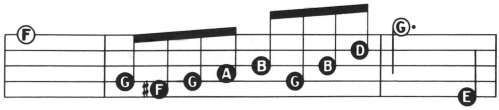

We're

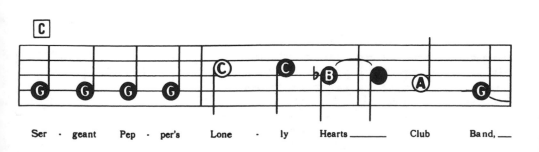

Ser · geant Pep · per's Lone - ly Hearts _____ Club Band, ___

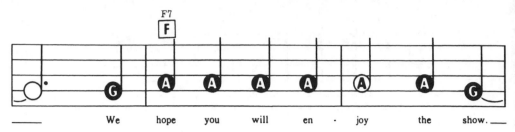

We hope you will en · joy the show.

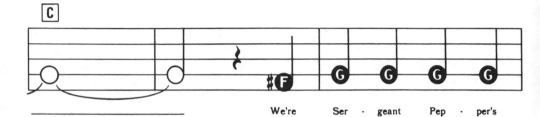

We're Ser · geant Pep · per's

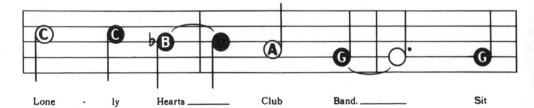

Lone · ly Hearts _____ Club Band. _____ Sit

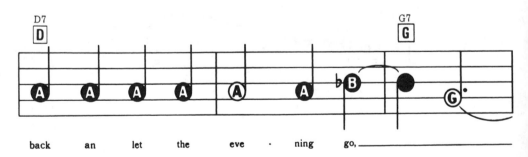

back an let the eve · ning go, _____

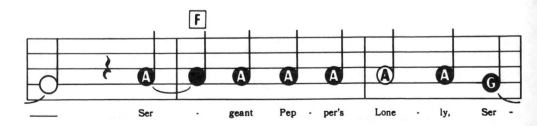

Ser · geant Pep · per's Lone · ly, Ser -

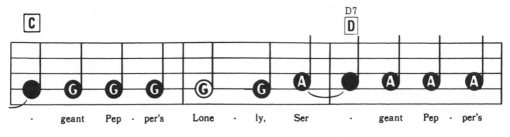

- geant Pep · per's Lone · ly, Ser · geant Pep · per's

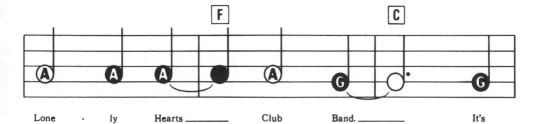

Lone · ly Hearts _____ Club Band. _____ It's

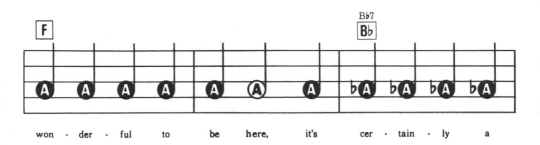

won · der · ful to be here, it's cer · tain · ly a

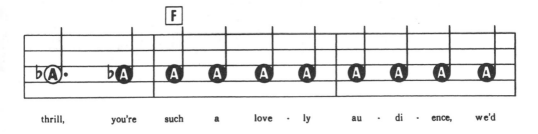

thrill, you're such a love · ly au · di · ence, we'd

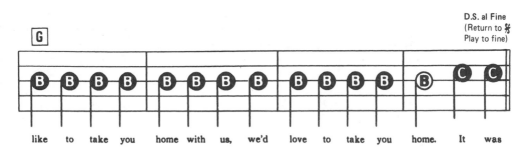

like to take you home with us, we'd love to take you home. It was

She's a Woman

Registration 3
Rhythm: Rock

Words and Music by John Lennon
and Paul McCartney

161

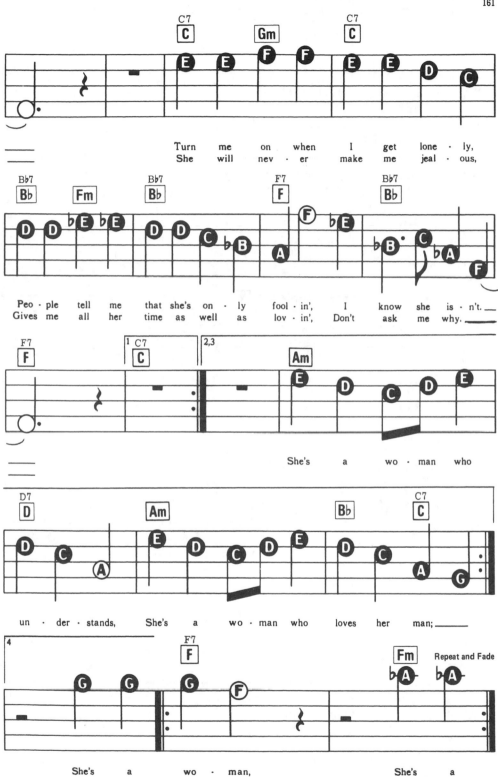

Something

Registration 4
Rhythm: Rock

Words and Music by
George Harrison

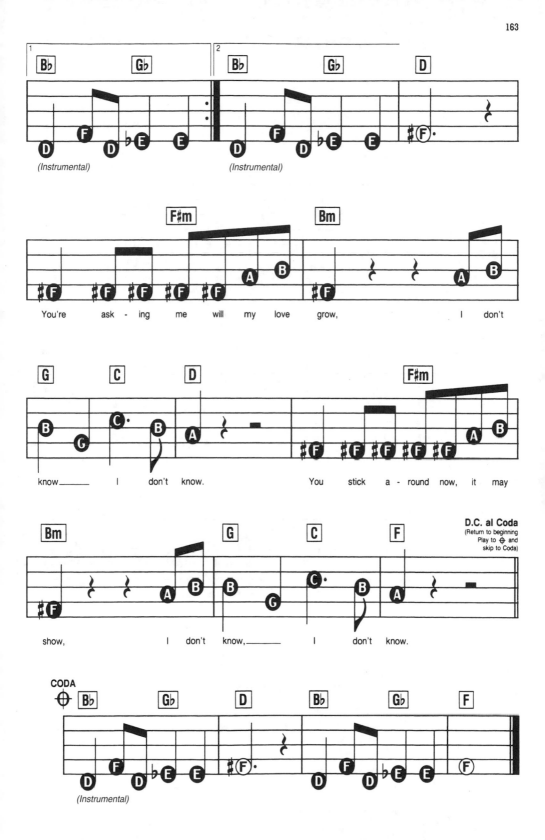

163

(Instrumental)

(Instrumental)

You're ask - ing me will my love grow, I don't

know____ I don't know. You stick a - round now, it may

show, I don't know,____ I don't know.

D.C. al Coda
(Return to beginning
Play to ⊕ and
skip to Coda)

CODA

(Instrumental)

Strawberry Fields Forever

Registration 2
Rhythm: Rock

Words and Music by John Lennon
and Paul McCartney

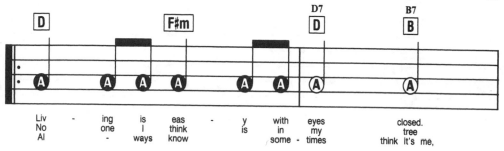

Liv - ing is eas - y with eyes closed.
No one I think is in my tree
Al - ways know some - times think it's me,

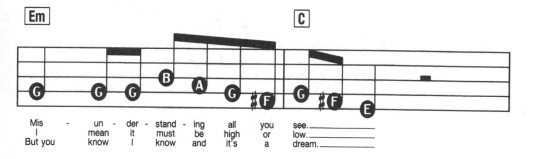

Mis - un - der - stand - ing all you see._____
I mean it must be high or low._____
But you know I know and it's a dream._____

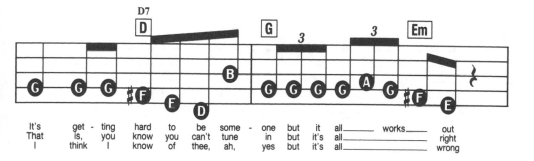

It's get - ting hard to be some - one but it all____ works____ out
That is, you know you can't tune in but it's all____ right
I think I know of thee, ah, yes but it's all____ wrong

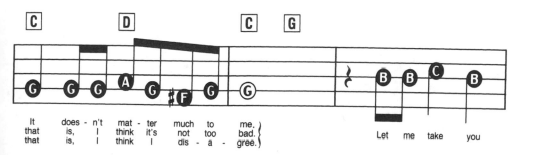

It does - n't mat - ter much to me.
that is, I think it's not too bad.
that is, I think I dis - a - gree.

Let me take you

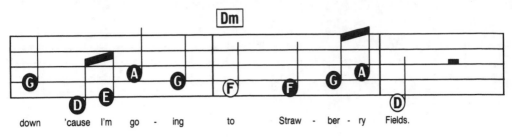

down 'cause I'm go - ing to Straw - ber - ry Fields.

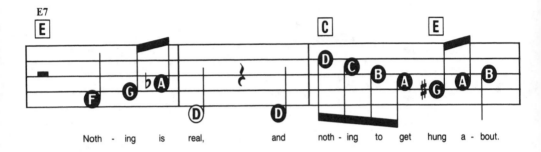

Noth - ing is real, and noth - ing to get hung a - bout.

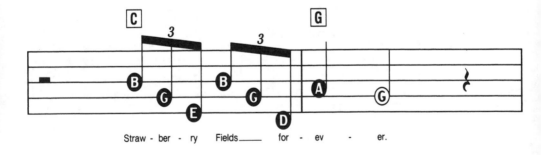

Straw - ber - ry Fields___ for - ev - er.

Repeat and Fade

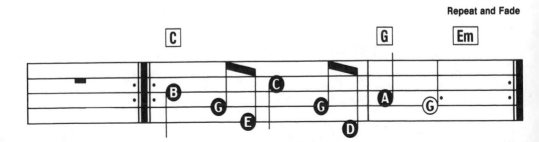

Twist and Shout

Registration 4
Rhythm: Rock

Words and Music by Bert Russell
and Phil Medley

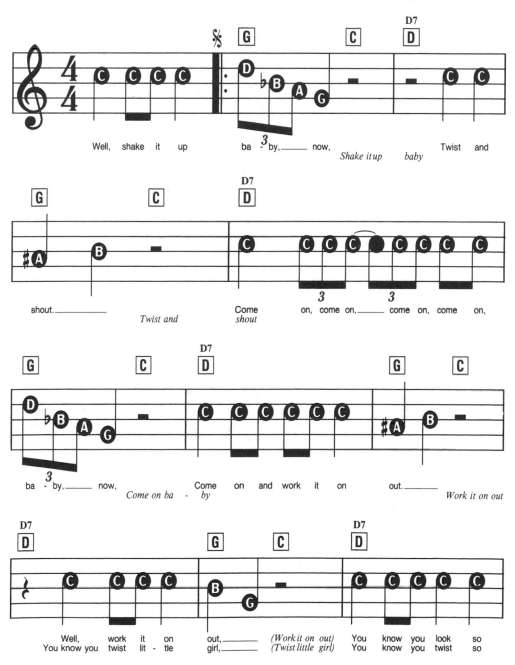

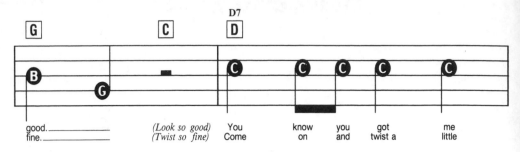

good._____ *(Look so good)* You know you got me
fine._____ *(Twist so fine)* Come on and twist a little

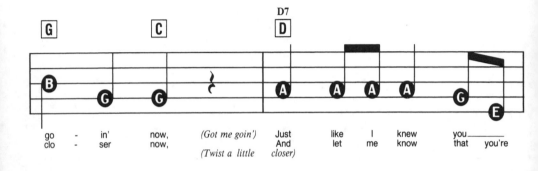

go - in' now, *(Got me goin')* Just like I knew you_____
clo - ser now, *(Twist a little closer)* And let me know that you're

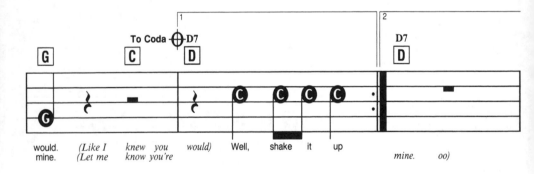

would. *(Like I knew you would)* Well, shake it up
mine. *(Let me know you're*

mine. oo)

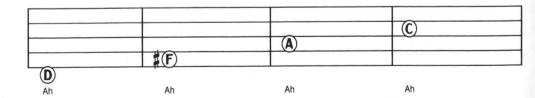

Ah   Ah   Ah   Ah

D.S. al Coda
(Return to §
Play to ⊕ and
skip to Coda)

CODA D7

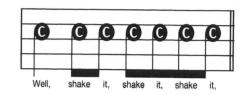

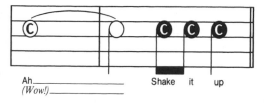

Ah_____
(Wow!)_____   Shake it up

Well, shake it, shake it, shake it,

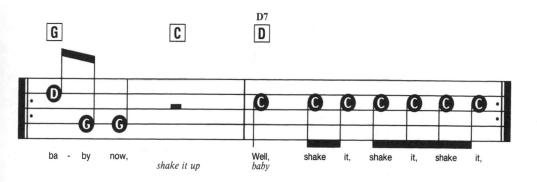

ba - by now,   *shake it up*   Well, shake it, shake it, shake it,
                              baby

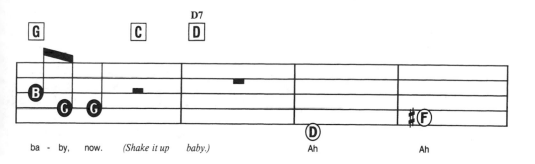

ba - by, now. *(Shake it up   baby.)*   Ah   Ah

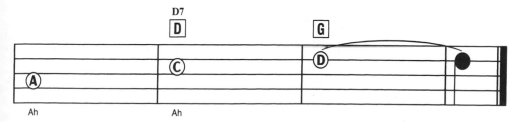

Ah   Ah

Taxman

Registration 2
Rhythm: Rock

Words and Music by
George Harrison

Let me tell you how it will be.
five per - cent what ap - pear will too be.
ask me what I want it small,

There's one for you, nine - teen for me.
Be thank - ful I don't take it all.
If you don't want to pay some more.

'Cause I'm the tax - man,

Yeh, _____ I'm the tax - man _____ Should tax - man.

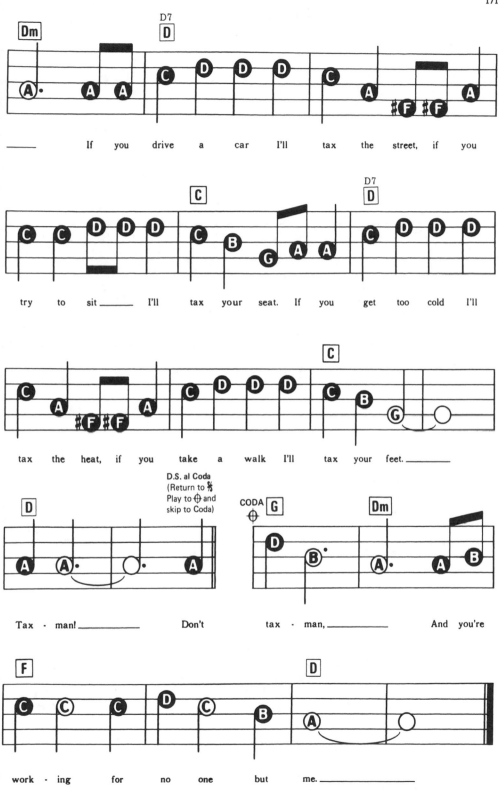

This Boy
(Ringo's Theme)

Registration 5
Rhythm: Slow Rock or Shuffle

Words and Music by John Lennon
and Paul McCartney

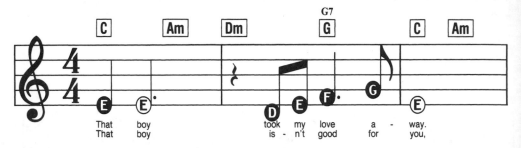

That boy   took my love a - way.
That boy   is - n't good for you,

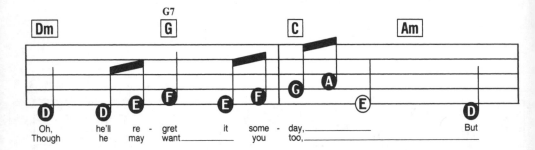

Oh,   he'll re - gret   it some - day,_____
Though   he may want_____   you too,_____   But

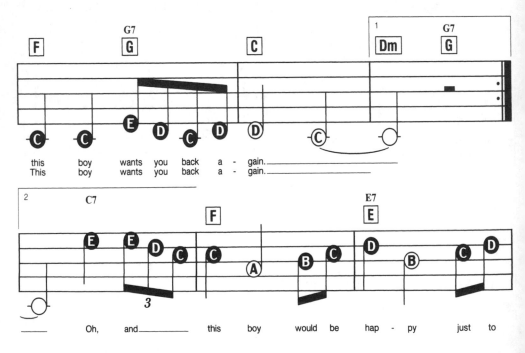

this   boy   wants you back a - gain._____
This   boy   wants you back a - gain._____

_____ Oh, and_____ this boy would be hap - py just to

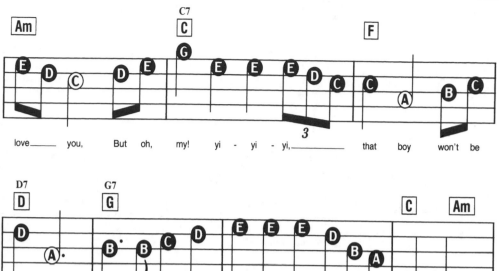

love___ you, But oh, my! yi - yi - yi,___ that boy won't be

hap - py till he's seen you cry, hi - hi - hi.___ This boy

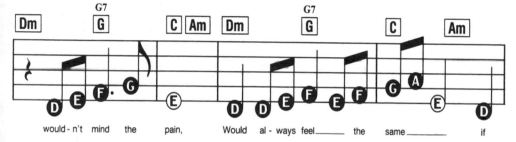

would - n't mind the pain, Would al - ways feel___ the same___ if

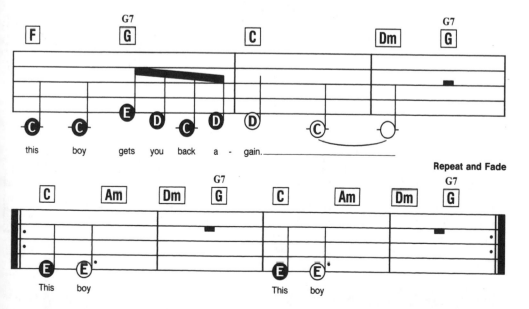

this boy gets you back a - gain.___

Repeat and Fade

This boy   This boy

Ticket to Ride

Registration 4
Rhythm: Rock

Words and Music by John Lennon
and Paul McCartney

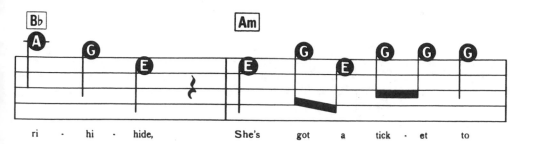

ri - hi - hide,   She's   got   a   tick - et   to

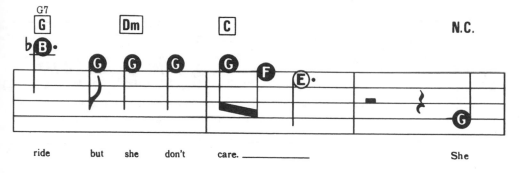

ride   but   she   don't   care. _____   She

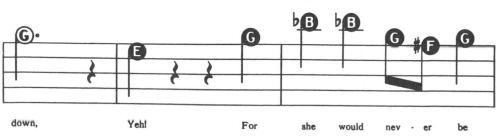

said   that   liv - ing   with   me   is   bring - ing   her

down,   Yeh!   For   she   would   nev - er   be

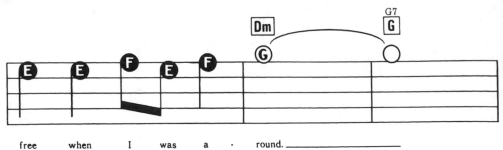

free   when   I   was   a - round. _____

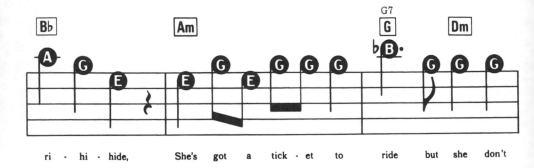

She's   got   a   tick - et   to   ride,   She's   got   a   tick - et   to

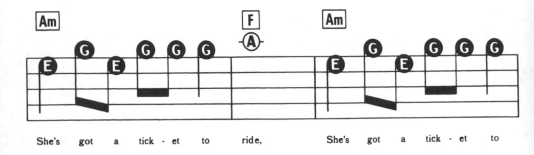

ri - hi - hide,   She's   got   a   tick - et   to   ride   but   she   don't

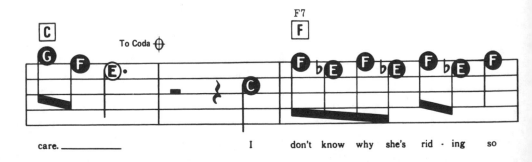

care. _____   I   don't   know   why   she's   rid - ing   so

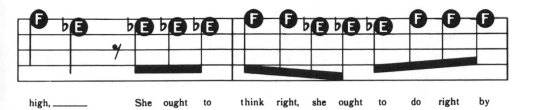

high, _____ She ought to think right, she ought to do right by

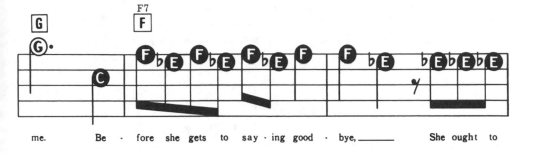

me. Be - fore she gets to say - ing good - bye, _____ She ought to

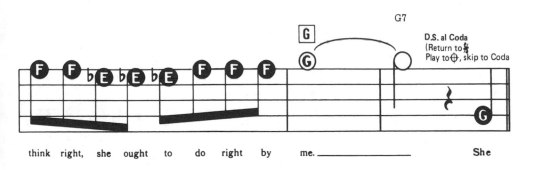

think right, she ought to do right by me. _____ She

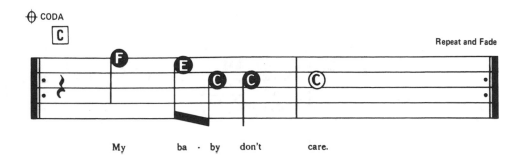

My ba - by don't care.

We Can Work It Out

Registration 9
Rhythm: Rock

Words and Music by John Lennon
and Paul McCartney

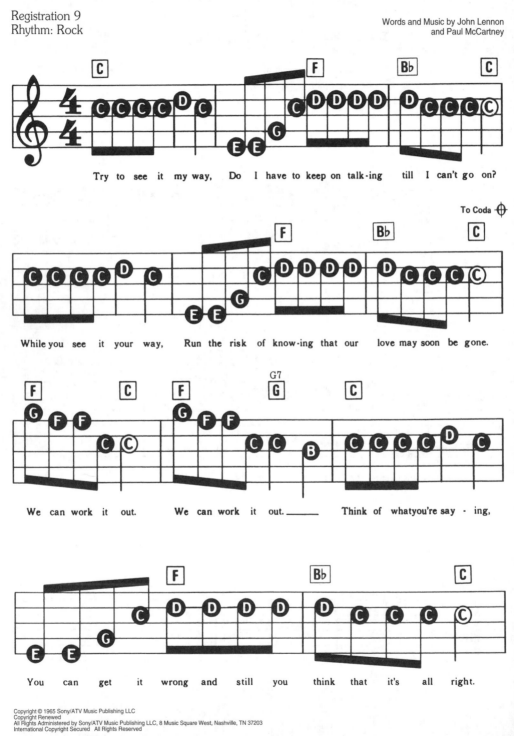

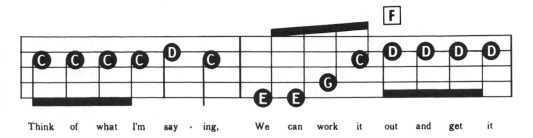

Think of what I'm say·ing, We can work it out and get it

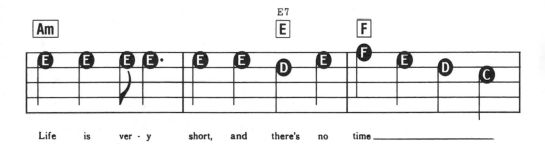

straight, or say good·night. We can work it out. We can work it out._____

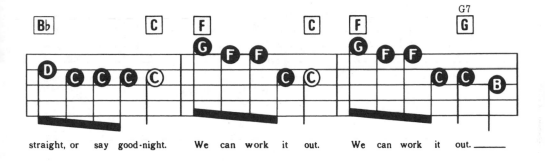

Life is ver·y short, and there's no time_____

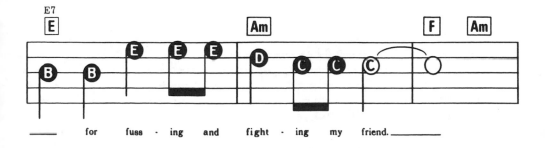

_____ for fuss·ing and fight·ing my friend._____

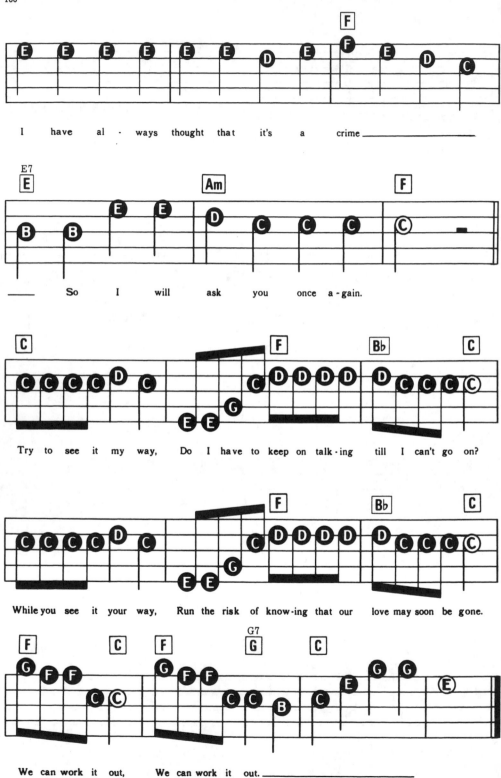

When I'm Sixty-Four

Registration 3
Rhythm: Rock

Words and Music by John Lennon
and Paul McCartney

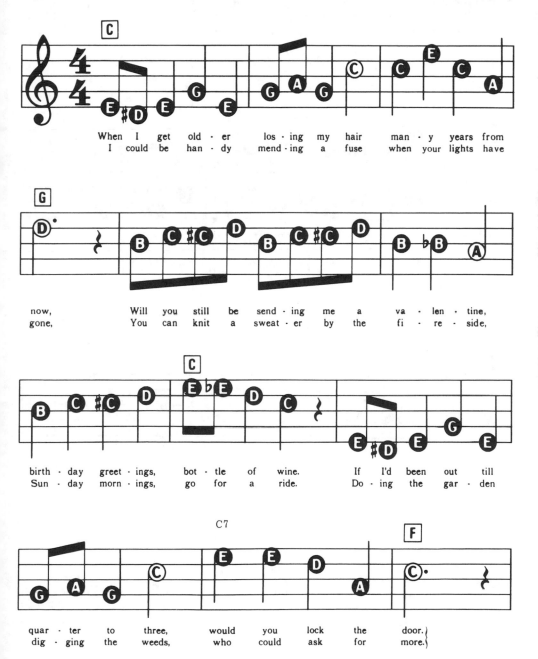

When I get old·er los·ing my hair man·y years from
I could be han·dy mend·ing a fuse when your lights have

now, Will you still be send·ing me a va·len·tine,
gone, You can knit a sweat·er by the fi·re·side,

birth·day greet·ings, bot·tle of wine. If I'd been out till
Sun·day morn·ings, go for a ride. Do·ing the gar·den

quar·ter to three, would you lock the door.
dig·ging the weeds, who could ask for more.

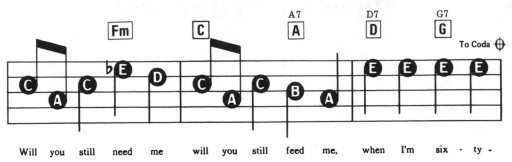

Will you still need me will you still feed me, when I'm six - ty -

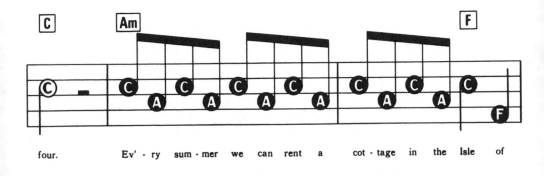

four. Ev' - ry sum - mer we can rent a cot - tage in the Isle of

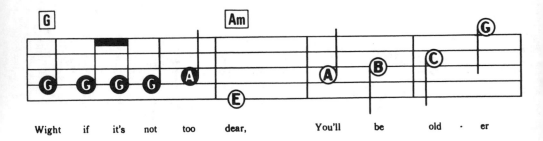

Wight if it's not too dear, You'll be old - er

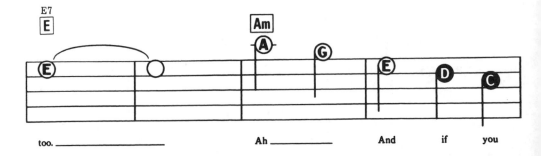

too. _____ Ah _____ And if you

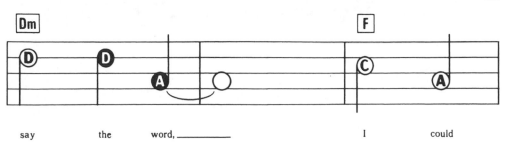

say the word,_____ I could

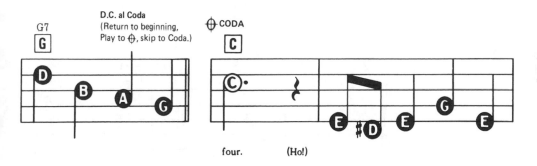

stay with you.

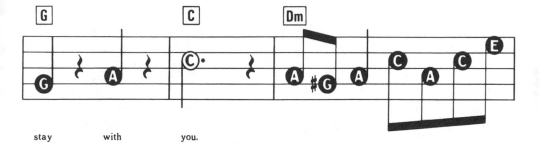

four. (Ho!)

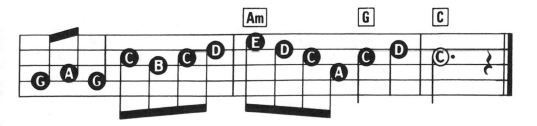

While My Guitar Gently Weeps

Registration 7
Rhythm: Rock or Latin

Words and Music by
George Harrison

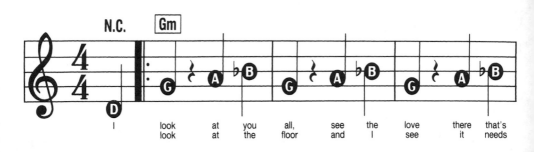

I look at you all, see the love there that's
look at the floor and I see it needs

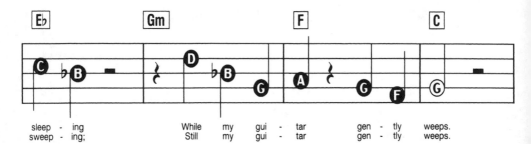

sleep - ing While my gui - tar gen - tly weeps.
sweep - ing; Still my gui - tar gen - tly weeps.

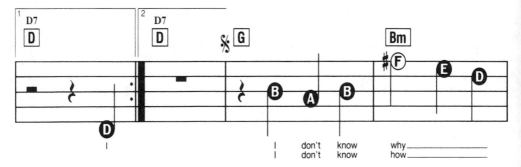

I
I don't know why
I don't know how

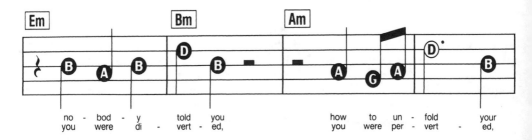

no - bod - y told you
you were di - vert - ed,

how to un - fold your
you were per - vert - ed,

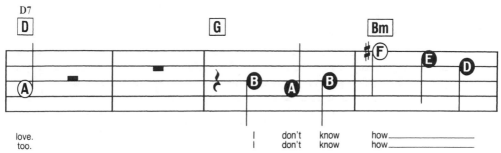

love.
too.

I don't know how_____
I don't know how_____

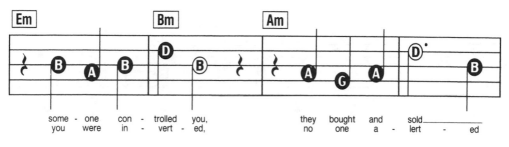

some - one con - trolled you,   they bought and sold_____
you were in - vert - ed,   no one a - lert - ed

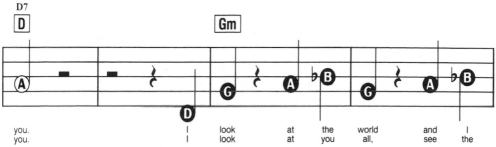

you.   I look at the world all, and I
you.   I look at the you see the

no - tice it's turn - ing   While my gui -
love there that's sleep - ing   While my gui -

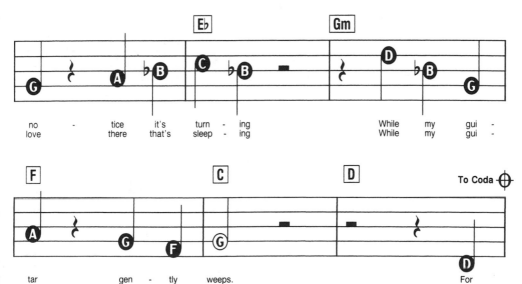

tar gen - tly weeps.   For
tar gen - tly weeps.

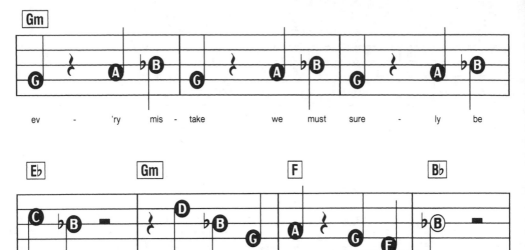

ev - 'ry mis - take we must sure - ly be

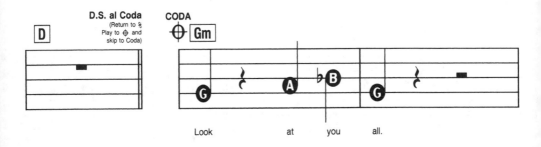

learn - ing; Still my gui - tar gen - tly weeps.

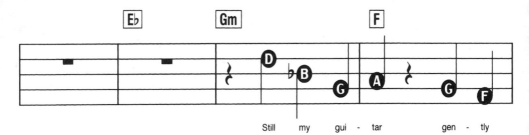

D.S. al Coda
(Return to %
Play to ⊕ and
skip to Coda)

CODA

Look at you all.

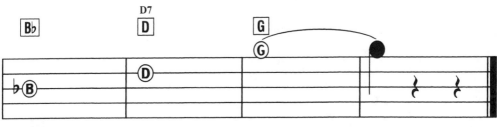

Still my gui - tar gen - tly

weeps.

With a Little Help from My Friends

Registration 5
Rhythm: Swing or Shuffle

Words and Music by John Lennon
and Paul McCartney

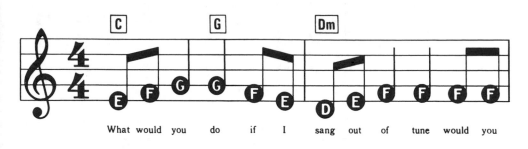

What would you do if I sang out of tune would you

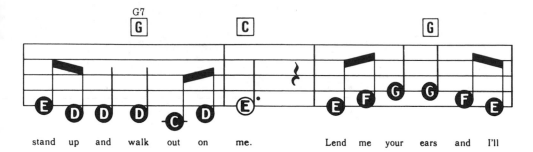

stand up and walk out on me. Lend me your ears and I'll

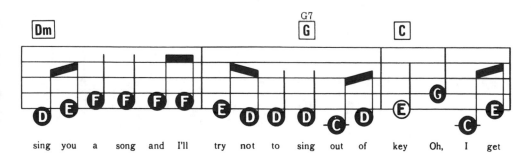

sing you a song and I'll try not to sing out of key Oh, I get

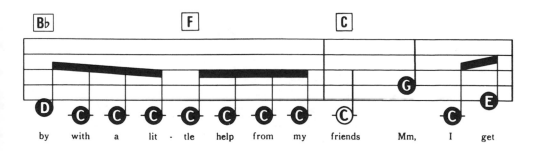

by with a lit-tle help from my friends Mm, I get

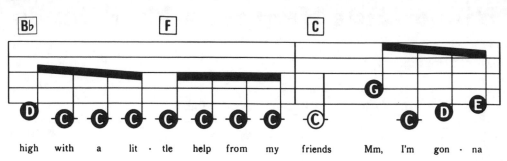

high with a lit‧tle help from my friends Mm, I'm gon‧na

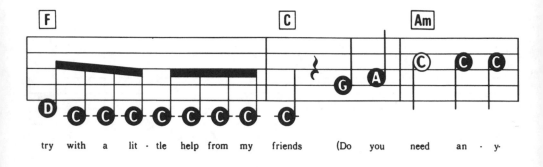

try with a lit‧tle help from my friends (Do you need an‧y‧

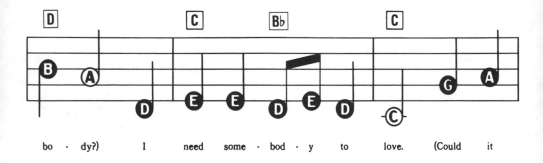

bo‧dy?) I need some‧bod‧y to love. (Could it

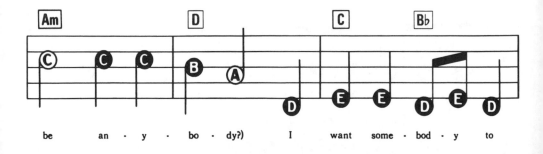

be an‧y‧bo‧dy?) I want some‧bod‧y to

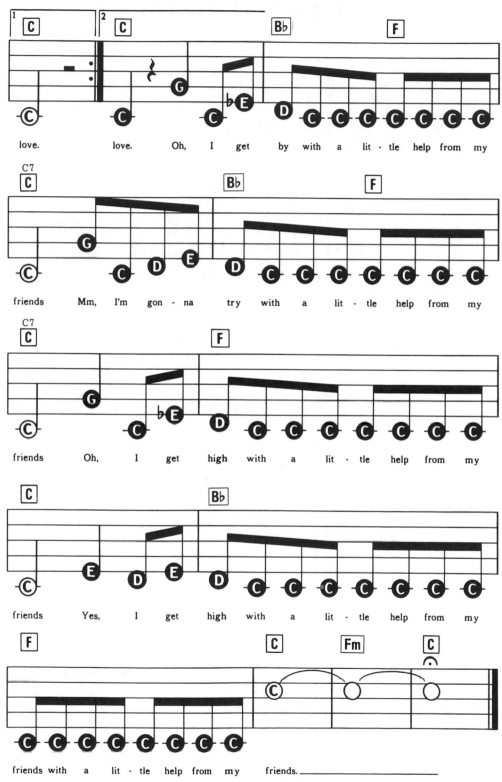

Yellow Submarine

Registration 2
Rhythm: 8 Beat or Rock

Words and Music by John Lennon
and Paul McCartney

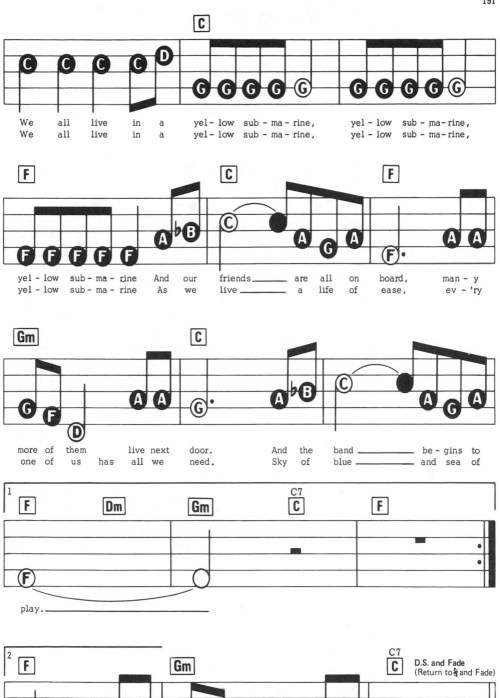

Yesterday

Registration 2
Rhythm: Rock or Ballad

Words and Music by John Lennon
and Paul McCartney

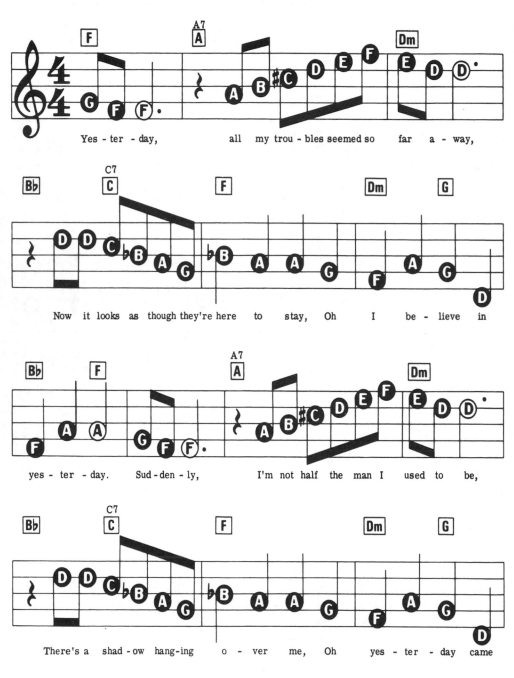

sud - den - ly.   Why   she   had   to   go   I   don't know,   she   would-n't

say.   I   said   some - thing wrong now I   long   for   yes - ter -

day._____   Yes - ter-day,   love was such an eas - y   game to   play.

Now I   need   a   place   to   hide   a - way,   Oh   I   be - lieve   in

yes - ter -day.   Mm - mm - mm - mm - mm - mm - mm._____

You Like Me Too Much

Registration 5
Rhythm: Rock

Words and Music by
George Harrison

Though you're gone a - way this morn - ing, you'll be
tried be - fore to leave me but you
I will fol - low you and bring you

back a - gain to - night, tell - ing me there'll be no
have - n't got the nerve to walk out and make me
back where you be - long 'Cause I could - n't real - ly

next time if I just don't treat you right. You'll
lone - ly which is all that I de - serve. You'll
stand it, I ad - mit that I was wrong, I

nev - er leave me and you know it's true, _____
nev - er leave me and you know it's true, _____
would - n't let you leave me 'cause it's true, _____

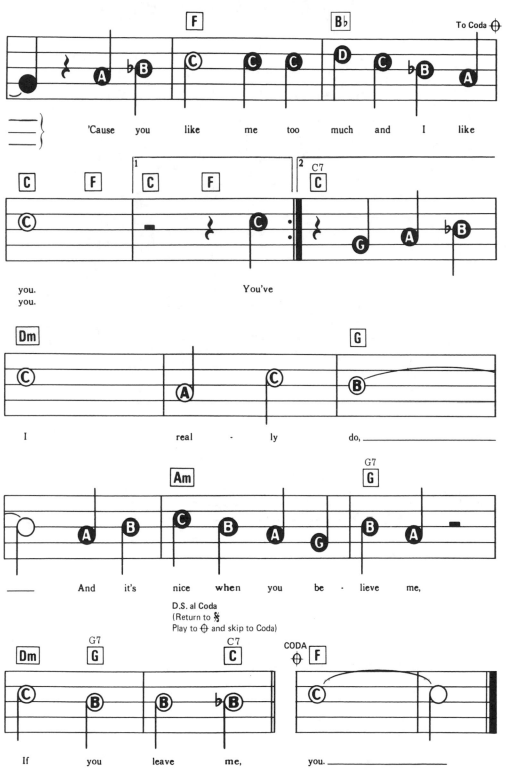

You Won't See Me

Registration 2
Rhythm: Rock

Words and Music by John Lennon
and Paul McCartney

When I call you up your line's _____ en -
know why you should want _____ to
days are few, they're filled _____ with

gaged; I have had e - nough so act _____ your
hide; but I had can't get through, my hands _____ are
tears; and since I lost you, it feels _____ like

age. We have lost the time that
tied. I won't want to stay, I
years. Yes, it seems so long

was so hard _____ to find; and I will lose my
don't have much _____ to say; and I can turn a -
since you've _____ been gone; and I just can't go

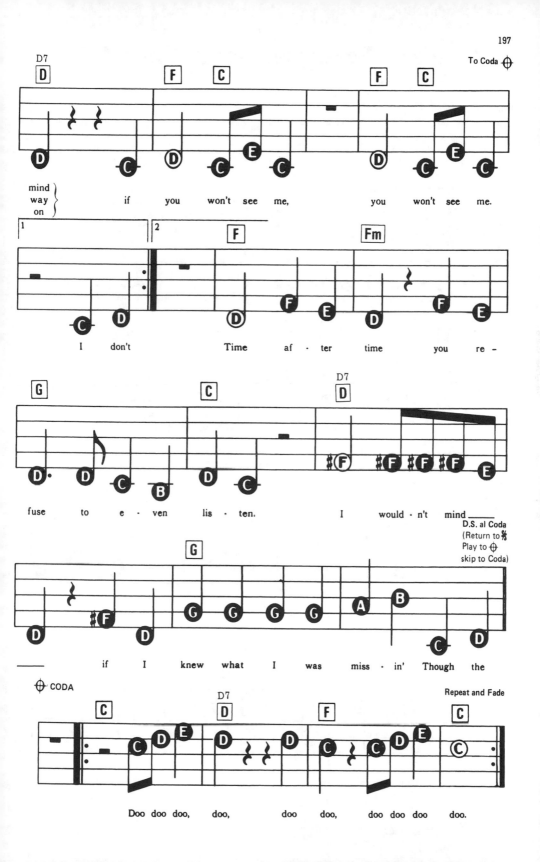

You're Going to Lose That Girl

Registration 4
Rhythm: Rock

Words and Music by John Lennon
and Paul McCartney

1,3 If you don't take her out to - night She's going to change her mind,
2. If you don't treat her right, my friend, You're going to find her gone,

And I will take her out to - night And I will treat her kind,
'Cause I will treat her right and then You'll be the lone - ly one,

You're going to lose that girl, You're going to

To Coda

lose that girl. _____ girl, _____ You're gon - na

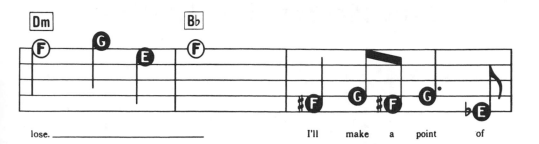

lose. _____ I'll make a point of

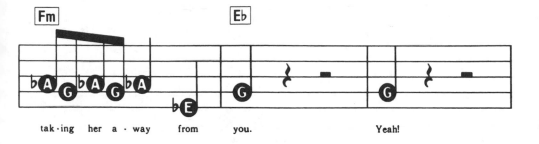

tak-ing her a - way from you. Yeah!

D.C. al Coda
(Return to the beginning
Play to ⊕ and skip to Coda)

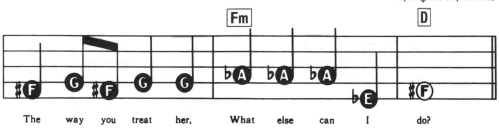

The way you treat her, What else can I do?

⊕ CODA

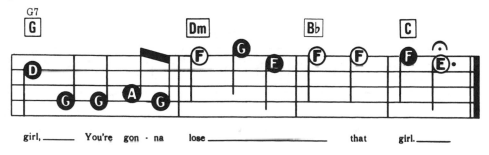

girl, _____ You're gon - na lose _____ that girl. _____

Your Mother Should Know

Registration 2
Rhythm: Rock or Shuffle

Words and Music by John Lennon
and Paul McCartney

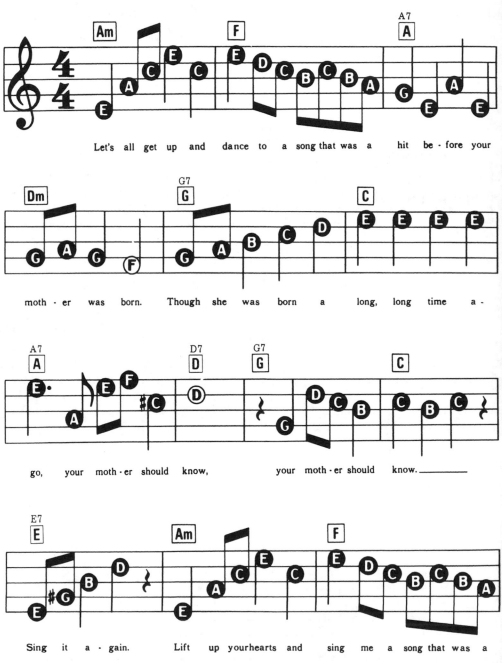

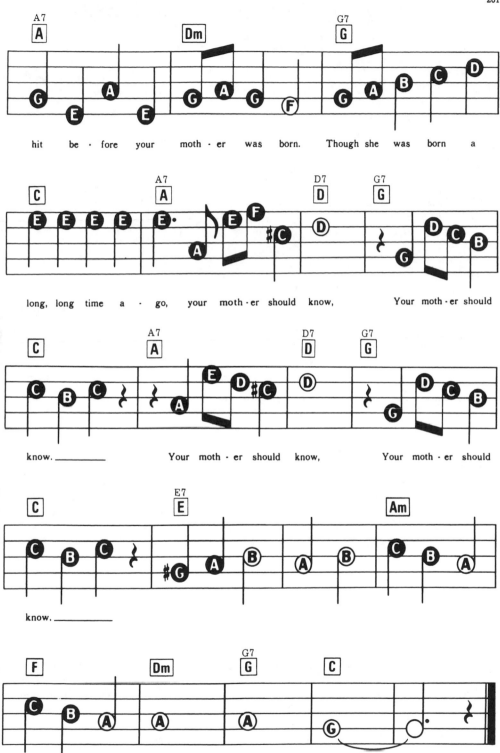

You've Got to Hide Your Love Away

Registration 4
Rhythm: Waltz

Words and Music by John Lennon
and Paul McCartney

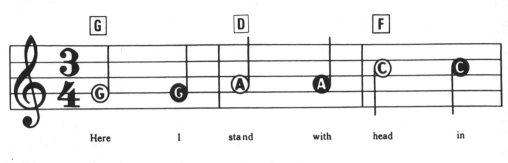

Here   I   stand   with   head   in

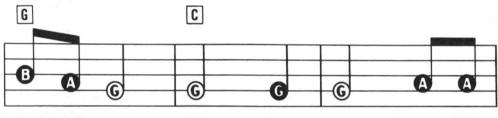

hand,_____   Turn   my   face   to   the

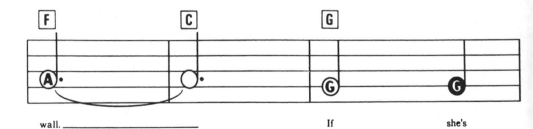

wall._____   If   she's

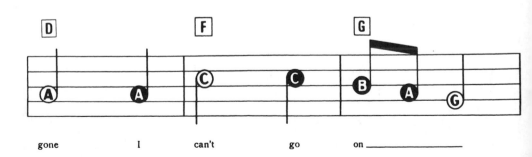

gone   I   can't   go   on _____

203

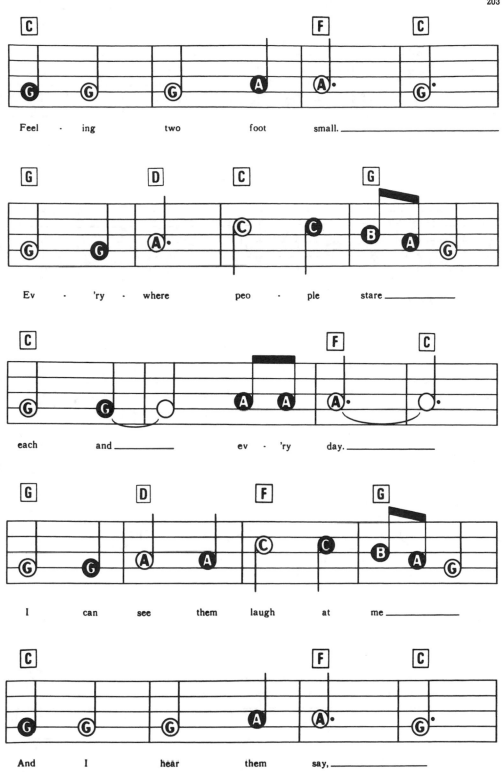

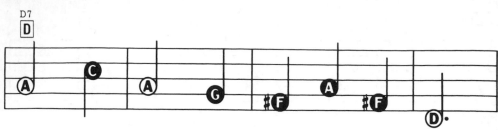

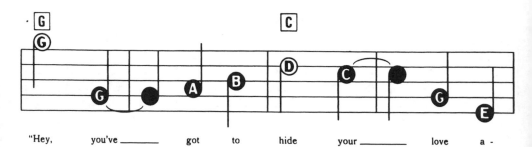

"Hey, you've _____ got to hide your _____ love a-

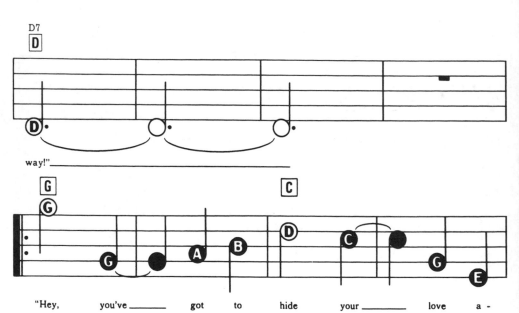

way!"_____

"Hey, you've _____ got to hide your _____ love a-

Repeat and Fade

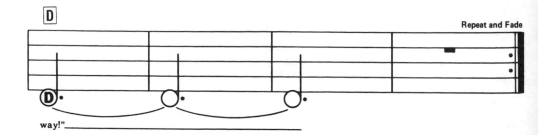

way!"_____